# HOW

# TECHNICAL DOCUMENTS

# HOW TO EDIT
# TECHNICAL DOCUMENTS

Donald W. Bush
and
Charles P. Campbell

Oryx Press
1995

*The rare Arabian Oryx is believed to have inspired the myth of the unicorn. This desert
antelope became virtually extinct in the early 1960s. At that time several groups of
international conservationists arranged to have 9 animals sent to the Phoenix Zoo
to be the nucleus of a captive breeding herd. Today the Oryx population
is over 1000, and over 500 have been returned to the Middle East.*

© 1995 by The Oryx Press
4041 North Central at Indian School Road
Phoenix, Arizona 85012-3397

Published simultaneously in Canada
Printed and Bound in the United States of America

∞ The paper used in this publication meets the minimum requirements of
American National Standard for Information Science—Permanence of Paper
for Printed Library Materials, ANSI Z39.48, 1984.

*Library of Congress Cataloging-in-Publication Data*

Bush, Donald W., 1925–
   How to edit technical documents / Donald W. Bush & Charles P.
Campbell.
      p.   cm.
   Includes bibliographical references and index.
   ISBN 0-89774-870-0 —ISBN 0-89774-964-2 (workbook)
   1. Technical editing.   I. Campbell, Charles P.   II. Title.
T11.4.B87   1995
808'.0666—dc20                                          95-9705
                                                            CIP

# CONTENTS

# PREFACE

This book differs significantly from others on technical editing in two ways. First, it concentrates on the difficult problem of editing technical content (often labeled, somewhat turgidly, "substantive editing"). Second, it attempts to apply the technology of English—some of the newer, practical precepts of rhetoric, linguistics, and semantics—to the problems of editing and getting along with authors.

"Technical editing," much like "technical writing," is an amorphous and ill-defined term. It applies mostly to editing done on technical reports, ranging from sales-oriented new-business proposals to the more academic journal articles, but it can also include work done on almost any kind of expository prose found in industry, and it can be applied with almost any degree of attention and expertise. Today, a prime emphasis is on user manuals, published in a hurry to try to coincide with the issuance of new software programs.

As amazing as it might seem to outsiders, many technical editors do not try to understand the content of the material they edit. In some offices, editors exist only to impose "consistency" in spelling, grammar, capitalization, and hyphenation. Much of the work is "Nintendo editing": using style-checking software to zap errors. Typically, these low-paid editors follow only rigid style manual rules, paying little attention to technical accuracy or, ironically, even to communication.

This narrow interpretation of "editing" not only denigrates the profession but also deprives companies and authors of the help they desperately need to make their new-business proposals sell, their user manuals instruct, and their technical papers achieve professional impact.

This book seeks to upgrade technical editing from today's automatic wrist-slapping to a thoughtful process that applies brains and common sense. Editors need to learn to trim copy to get authors to the point quicker, and to develop continuity, paragraph coherence, and overall organization. These are tasks that can't be accomplished with software.

This means, of course, that editors will have to be smarter than before; they will have to learn to make their own decisions. But the rewards will be commensurate with the upgrading of the duties.

Potentially, good editors can work miracles. They can turn the prevailing turgidity and obfuscation of technical writing into authoritative, convincing, selling prose. Moreover, they can cut costs drastically, simply by reducing the intimidating size of today's documentation.

## GETTING TO KNOW THE AUTHORS

Unfortunately, technical editing today often takes place in isolation. An editor of software user manuals, proposals, technical reports, and journal articles may sit in his or her own room, down the hall from the subject experts, or even across the campus or across the country. Sometimes editors are mixed in with the keyboarders, occasionally even exchanging duties with them. Editors may not know the authors personally or understand what they are trying to say.

Too often, too, the writer-editor relationship is combative. The editors pride themselves on being "language police" and eagerly swing their billy clubs against the proudly crafted prose of over-sensitive technical authors.

Obviously, a better editing approach is to try to find out what the author wants to say and help him say it. This friendly technique leads to better relations, too, with those other friends, the readers.

## THE TECHNOLOGY OF ENGLISH

In most professions—say, medicine, or fire protection—practitioners are eager to apply the newest technology. Technical editors, however, too often confine their expertise to high school grammar and the pronouncements of the style manual, ignoring what experts are learning today about language. Even textbooks on technical editing rely mostly on hammering home concepts that the subject experts once learned in school themselves.

Thus today, technical editing is left with no body of knowledge. Sadly, this means that employers can fill job openings from a pool of majors in philosophy, psychology, foreign languages, journalism, religion, drama, etc. (Experience shows that some of the best current technical editors were music majors.) Today, the main requirement cited in the "technical editor" want-ads is typing, along with facility in the current desktop publishing software. Our body of knowledge is coming to be keyboarding.

This book tries to show how technical editing can improve itself by employing the technology of English. By this, we mean practical, tested techniques that apply what the academic world and experienced editors know about language. We're not talking about concepts derived from advertising, journalism, and marketing as much as from elementary rhetoric, linguistics, semantics, and transformational grammar. Knowing their own

English technology will allow editors to bring something to the table, rather than learning their information transfer from the engineers, who don't always have it right (Bush 1992).

## PRACTICAL APPLICATIONS

The ideas in this book, if new to many technical editors, are not difficult.

For instance, we try to show new editors how to read and understand technical copy. The key turns out to be structure. As demonstrated in our accompanying workbook, a good editor can structure even nonsense words into an effective order, as in Lewis Carroll's "Jabberwocky."

We also try to show the overwhelming advantages of cutting copy (Brogan 1973). Perhaps the greatest fault of technical writing is that there is simply too much of it. The messages become terribly hard to understand, and supervisors, striving to explain them better, add still more sentences. This choking proliferation of wordage delays both publication and assimilation. Some of our principles of word economy were mined from Joseph M. Williams (1994), while others have come from our experience in "cutting things out without cutting anything out" (Bush 1994).

The book argues that an editor should follow a linguistics approach (Read 1989). In technical editing, this approach means working primarily with structure while "letting the experts have their words" (Bush 1993). The theory turns out to be popular with technical authors, too.

Technical jargon is not all bad (Crabtree 1991). According to Philip Howard (1985), it is Janus-oriented, some of it being very good for conveying technical thoughts to technical people. Most of the charges of "you changed my meaning" simply indicate that a well-meaning editor has removed some vital technical jargon.

The book specifically attempts to show how to help the subject expert (SE) communicate while fostering support rather than antagonism. We believe that the solution is not ardent attention to rules but rather a flexible, knowledgeable application of solid principles of communication. Editing can also be an effective teaching tool; it shows the experts how they can improve their writing next time.

The book also addresses organization. Technical documents in general are poorly organized, but few editing textbooks attack this difficult problem. We urge editors not to fall back on the traditional SE favorites of "chronological" or "alphabetical" order, but instead use "macroediting" techniques to look at the whole composition and derive logical groupings, hierarchies, and sequences, as though they were editing a film. This is not as difficult as it might seem, because using "deductive" patterns appropriate to expository writing is very helpful (Winterowd 1975).

The book tries to apply the often-misunderstood study of general semantics to combat the literal, "one word, one meaning" dicta of technically oriented people. We think that S. I. Hayakawa (1990), a highly respected but easy-to-read authority on semantics, also has a lot to say to editors about classification and abstraction and also language bias.

Incidentally, as an aid to spelling, we have included the fascinating etymology of selected technical words.

To improve the sentence, which we call the "idea module," we advance the theme-rheme concept (see, for instance, Walpole 1979), which was effectively revived by George Gopen and Judith Swan (1990). This concept brings emphasis out of dullness, and can be extended to enhance continuity between sentences and even paragraphs. We also try to show how little tricks of sequencing words properly can make sentences smoother and more idiomatic, and therefore more understandable.

The paragraph may be the single most neglected writing device in technical editing instruction. In this book, we treat paragraphs not from the writer's viewpoint, as building blocks, but as the editor sees them: parts of the whole and valuable organizing devices for the reader.

We approach grammar in two ways, both of them stemming from advanced English study. For analysis, we use transformational grammar (Morenberg 1991, Kolln 1994, Kaplan 1989), which is the outgrowth of revolutionary studies by Noam Chomsky (1957). This approach easily leads to descriptive, rather than prescriptive, grammar (Finegan 1980, Baron 1982, Burchfield 1991). Descriptive grammar confirms that educated readers no longer worry much about rules against (say) splitting the infinitive, but more about ultimate meaning. This is not a new approach, but a distinctly unusual one for technical editing.

Similarly, the book employs medieval practice on one hand and transformational grammar on the other to demonstrate the help offered the reader by somewhat extensive punctuation.

The discussion of visuals advocates not color and "prettiness," but the synergetic help offered to the reader by text, art, and overall design (White 1982 and 1990). It also examines some of the imaginative ideas of Tufte (1983 and 1990) and the on-line expertise of Horton (1990 and 1991) and Price (1984 and 1993).

## AIMS OF THE BOOK

As stated, the main goal of the book is to try to upgrade the technical editing profession, allowing it to realize its full potential as a tool for communication and to act as a bridge between the "two cultures" (Snow 1959).

We have aimed first at technical editing students, trying to show them how to apply language expertise to attain a more valuable, more satisfying career. However, we also want to reach technical supervisors who want to learn how to do one of their most important and time-consuming jobs: improving the writing of their people. Another important audience is managers who have a pressing need to improve the writing in their departments while reducing document size and preparation time and cost.

And finally, the book may be ideal for English teachers, who may be pleased to find practicable applications of the "technology of English" in the world of work.

You, the readers, are the best judge of our book. If you have comments, please drop a note to The Oryx Press, especially if you find spots where we violate our own advice.

# ACKNOWLEDGEMENTS

Thanks to Prof. Scott P. Sanders, University of New Mexico, for getting us together to write this book, and to Herbert B. Michaelson for bringing us to Oryx.

Thanks to our wives, Ramona Bush and Tommi Campbell, who helped us through intense periods of writing.

Thanks to the Society for Technical Communication for permission to reprint portions of Don Bush's "The Friendly Editor" columns in *Technical Communication* that were reworked into various chapters.

Thanks to the Institute of Electrical and Electronic Engineers for permission to rework parts of Charles P. Campbell's "Engineering Style: Striving for Efficiency" [*IEEE Transactions on Professional Communication* 35 (September 1992)] that now appear in Chapters 6 and 7.

Thanks to the many who, wittingly or unwittingly, have contributed text specimens.

And not least, thanks to Susan Slesinger and Sean Tape at Oryx for carefully reading the manuscript and making many helpful suggestions. Editors, when they write, need editors, too.

# HOW TO EDIT
# TECHNICAL DOCUMENTS

# CHAPTER

**A**n editor is someone who ~~changes~~ ~~alters~~ ~~amends~~ improves other people's writing. A technical editor is likely to do this on (1) material that is technical (i.e., material that contains specialized or quantitative information, some of it in graphs, tables, or equations) or (2) material that is generated in organizations that do technical work.

The goal of editing is to make documents more understandable for readers, who are clients and customers—the people whose continuing satisfaction is crucial to the survival of the companies.

To help these readers, editors need a solid foundation in the workings of language. They need the skills appropriate to producing documents both with and without computer technology, and they need to understand some principles of visual design and text layout. But the core of what technical editors do is to work with language, and that is what we emphasize in this book.

The centrality of language has been somewhat eclipsed in recent years by the fascination with computers. The computer software industry has provided employment for legions of technical writers and editors who, in turn, are expected to use computers as tools for working with documentation. Indeed, computers can now do certain things more reliably than human editors, such as search-and-replace, spellcheck, and point out wordy or passive constructions.

## EDITORS' RESPONSIBILITIES TO THE AUDIENCE

Technical editors are burdened with a variety of responsibilities:
- to their organization
- to the reader
- to the author
- to the language

# Technical Editing: A Changing Profession

✍

**An editor is someone who ~~changes~~ ~~alters~~ ~~amends~~ improves other people's writing.**

**Responsibilities (Some-
times Conflicting) of
Technical Editors**

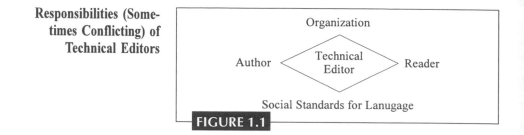

FIGURE 1.1

This relationship is shown in Figure 1.1.

The most obvious responsibility to the organization is for the editor to do a day's work for a day's pay. Less obvious, and less easy, is the responsibility to act for the greater good of the company.

Companies sometimes employ editors to do tasks that don't use editors' skills to the best advantage. Also, editors are sometimes overruled by authors, or they may be frustrated by rigid guidelines on document design. Management often establishes a policy and expects everybody to abide by it, even though it may not serve the company's best interests.

Authors also may have responsibilities tugging them in several directions. They are usually writing for several audiences at once, and, as Mathes and Stevenson (1991) have shown, they may go astray if they think that the audience for their report is the supervisor who handed them the assignment.

In Mathes and Stevenson's terms, the supervisor is only the immediate audience for the report, whereas the *primary* audience is made up of those who use the findings. There is also likely to be a secondary audience of readers who are affected by the decisions of the primary audience.

Authors, being focused on technical matters, often fail to realize that they are writing for these multiple audiences. They also often assume that readers will have background and expertise similar to their own. And they may get their backs up when editors, who make good surrogates for audiences, question whether a document will actually meet audience needs.

Most organizations never let authors get near the audience. An exception, we've heard, is a software company that has its writers answer customer-service telephones: dealing with grumpy customers gives them a sense of audience that is very immediate.

## FAULTY ANALOGIES FOR EDITORS

The effectiveness of editors in satisfying the needs of their audiences depends a lot on how editors see themselves.

One editor had gained the confidence of a technical group in a large company. Leaving the publications department to join the group, he played an important role in helping the technical specialists design the documentation of projects at the proposal stage. His role was akin to that of a managing editor in publishing: he was able to concentrate on the shape and content of the documentation and supervise the copyediting that was farmed out to the firm's publications department. He found the work enjoyable and rewarding.

Then one day the leader of one of the big projects paid the editor this compliment: "You know, you're really important in this group. You're like its anal sphincter—we pass all this [expletive deleted] down the pipe to you, and you give it shape and solidity so it comes out looking great."

The analogy forever changed that editor's view of his work. Not long afterward, he accepted an ill-paid position as an instructor in a small college.

A similarly discouraging analogy likens the editor to a janitor: after the authors have done the "real work," the editor comes along and tidies up.

This sort of thinking, no doubt, was responsible for the recent plight of another editor. Mary worked for a defense-contracting branch of a large industrial corporation. She worked in the publications department, which was separated by a wall from the engineering department. Work was handed in through a window. Editors corrected English and conformed the documents to military specifications. But because they had no contact with engineers, no one on the technical side understood what they did, so when a contract was lost and the workforce had to be reduced, the company dismissed Mary and 40 other editors.

## COLLABORATIVE USES OF EDITOR'S SKILLS

There are more useful functions for editors than janitorial ones. Here are a few examples.

Stan works for a large corporation in a division that develops software for business applications. Documentation must be ready to ship with the software, so technical writers are developing it even before programmers have finished writing the code. Stan works with a company style guide, set up in a computer format, to put sections into a predetermined format. Whenever possible, Stan acts as a reader advocate by attempting to follow the instructions written by the technical writers.

Gloria works for a contract engineering firm, acting as the focal point for its proposal writing. She talks to the client's contract people to understand the client's need and see what standards proposals must meet. She draws together technical material prepared by the engineering staff and massages "boilerplate" (prewritten descriptions of the company, its previous work, and its professional staff) into cohesive and persuasive writing. Her formal title, however, is "proposals coordinator."

George works for a large consulting firm that puts together ad hoc teams of experts—market researchers, engineers, operations researchers, economists—to work on projects that are likely to have large public impact. Acting as an aide to project leaders, he takes part in team meetings, beginning with the proposal and continuing throughout the life of the project. He helps develop the document plan and schedule, develops a project style sheet, collects the inputs from professional staff, supervises graphic artists and other editors, and coordinates production.

Ruth, with many years' seniority in a government laboratory, specializes in heavily editing the writing from research scientists to create slick reports that are used to explain the laboratory's mission and progress to the public (and particularly to congressional budget committees). Because this work demands that Ruth understand the science and the audience in order to create the bridge between them, Ruth has been asked to work full time to help the public understand why the laboratory's work should continue in the face of shrinking budgets. She is now called a "public relations specialist."

In industry and government, many tasks that fall to editors don't seem to have much to do with "correcting copy." That's all some technical editors do, but it's not all they can do.

Committed career editors and upwardly mobile editors alike often have to convince managers and technical specialists that there is more to editing than imposing company style and shepherding documents through production. An editor's scope depends on the degree of trust she has earned from her technical colleagues.

---

### WHAT EDITING ISN'T

1. Editing is *not* writing. But an editor should be a good writer.
2. Editing is *not* copyreading. But an editor must catch all mistakes in grammar, spelling, and punctuation.
3. Editing is *not* just a consistency check. But an editor can't allow sloppy capitalization, hyphenation, etc.
4. Editing is certainly *not* proofreading. But an editor had better not miss any typos.
5. Editing is *not* just following the style book blindly. In fact, it's often making the style book match the edited copy.
6. Editors *cannot* be responsible for the accuracy of content, but they must make accuracy their first responsibility.
7. Editing is *not* personnel management. But an editor must get along with artists and printers. And other editors.
8. Editing means *not* compromising standards. But an editor must not tread on the toes of an author.
9. Editing is certainly *not* layout. But the editor's name may be on the masthead.
10. Editing is *not* publications management. But cost overruns are dealt with severely.
11. Editing is *not* just soliciting articles. An editor must also guide their writing.
12. Editing is *not* planning. But it's close.

## TECHNICAL EDITING AS A CAREER

For a technical editor, advancement depends on her evident usefulness. To cultivate among scientists and engineers the idea that she is useful and get the chance to do more than police consistency, a neophyte editor may need to make her presence known.

It helps to show a willingness to learn about the technical fields. Asking lots of questions is one approach to becoming an overnight expert.

Most important, however, a new editor should be prepared with the technical knowledge of her own field. She should know how to argue forcefully about grammar, usage, audience needs, rhetorical strategy, document organization, and readability.

Often, scientists and engineers feel insecure about their language skills, and many welcome the help of an editor who knows her way around the *Harbrace Handbook*. But, as the editor comes to be seen as someone having a professional competence beyond correcting spelling and grammar, she will be entrusted with more interesting tasks.

A senior technical editor or technical writer—some firms don't maintain a sharp distinction—may be called on to help put together a proposal, and then, if a contract is awarded, to work with the project leader in laying out the schedule and outline for the periodic reports to keep the work on course.

An outline helps team members write their individual sections so that they fit into the whole without extensive reworking. Such an outline introduces some order into the process, but there are still enough variations in team members' interpretations to require the editor to do heavy editing or substantial revision.

Even before a draft report is complete, an editor will likely have gotten technical illustrators busy on the artwork and arranged for typesetting (if the firm has not yet converted to desktop publishing), as well as for printing and binding. Sometimes, with a tight deadline, the editor will also make arrangements for overnight shipping.

As the firm grows and her own role prospers, an editor may even fill a role similar to that of a general editor in the publishing industry, in charge of a stable of editors and concerned with production facilities, publication budgets, hiring, and seeing that all of the company's reports are done well and on time.

No matter where they work, editors do much more than correct grammar. Their coordination skills are so important that, in writing his guidelines for new editors, Annett (1985), an English teacher, does not even mention text-working skills; instead, his guidelines list only the qualities an editor needs in order to work with authors.

Author–editor relations can easily become strained under the enormous pressure of deadlines. An author who has just spent 36 hours locked up with a mountain of notes and a computer terminal isn't likely to respond politely to a young editor's criticism of the author's faulty predication in a tone that suggests the author shouldn't have been allowed to pass fifth grade.

Now, with the shift from the linear production model to desktop publishing, some editors have become more like writing coaches than copy correctors; their value lies not so much in their ability to catch punctuation errors as in their skill at collaborating simultaneously with several dozen subject experts.

## THE CHANGING NATURE OF TECHNICAL EDITORS' WORK

In the hierarchy of documentation preparation, there are, first, the managers who decide what documentation is necessary; next, the subject experts who provide the input; then, the technical writers; then the editors; and then the production people who do the keyboarding, drawing, photography, platemaking, printing, and binding.

The flow of work in this model used to be entirely linear. Editors' marking was done for the benefit of the person who had to re-keyboard the manuscript. Hence were developed standard marking symbols: the production-line orientation necessitated standardization. Any keyboarder needed to be able to interpret the marks made by any editor. And within the assembly-line production model, editors had certain well-defined responsibilities, many of them analogous to quality-control functions on the production line.

While the production-line model may never be entirely superseded, a number of developments are causing it to change significantly. Many of these developments are connected to computer technology—not just hardware and software, but the ways of thinking that attend them.

First, in industry we are seeing more and more "production teams" and "quality circles." The byword is *collaboration.*

Until now, no one has been very fond of "collaborative editing," in which groups sit around a table and discuss each sentence, and sometimes each word, until far into the night. Most professional editors will feign a sudden attack of cholera to avoid a conference like that, recovering the next day, of course, in time to fix the over-qualified statements and labyrinthine sentences that typically result.

Industry has always had the approval cycle, the epitome of sequential collaboration. But we now need to find ways to collaborate simultaneously, so we can swap ideas and brainstorm problems. We perhaps need to explore "blind" computer sessions, where ideas are thrown onto a screen anonymously, theoretically removing the heavy influence that inevitably attaches to statements by the boss.

Software is now providing us with various options for simultaneous computer editing: split screens, mark-throughs that preserve the original copy, storage devices that again preserve the original, and many other computerized methods of implementation, including identification of the marks of each editor/supervisor by color.

In one way, nothing has changed. Even simultaneous collaboration is not entirely new. For instance, multiple copies of proposals have always been routinely distributed, and supervisors at all levels have had the option of attacking the prose with their own color of pencil, the brighter the better.

But at the last roundup, good editors have been able to prevail, because (1) they find more mistakes, (2) they cut more superfluous wordage, and (3) they furnish better beginnings, better summations, and more graceful language throughout. Thus, the editor's copy is the one that most often survives as the "master," with only emendations by the others. (This is partly because few supervisors patiently edit clear to the end, venting most of their spleen on page 1.)

Now, with the computer, we may see more participation by top management. (It's easier and more fun than the old way of using pencils.) Also, the distribution of copies is potentially unlimited, inviting participation by hordes of eager amateurs of all ranks.

But the real problem is that there is no readily apparent way in a last roundup to look at several dozen copies simultaneously and select the best, combining comments of all the others. Technology has forced us back into a linear appraisal. Now the editing that survives is likely to be that of the highest ranking vice president, who spent her valuable time punching out corrections and expects to see them in the final version. Even the editor's carefully crafted suggestions may be deleted.

Each company will eventually find its own way to cope. Maybe it can limit distribution to three or four people. Maybe it can assign a competent editor to the slow process of sitting in with the vice president and helping her edit (until the vice president gets too busy and gives the editor her authority).

But perhaps the happiest solution is for the editor to become so well established that he is trusted by the entire company to accept comments and meld them into a smooth document for final approval. This will take up *his* valuable time. (He has to edit the draft, too.) But if he gets too pressed, perhaps he will be awarded an assistant.

## CONTRACT WORK

Companies are becoming smaller, less monolithic, and less stable. More and more, to smooth the peaks and valleys and also to avoid paying fringe benefits, they are relying on temporary workers, tied to the company not for the long range, but only by finite contracts.

Contract work is certainly nothing new for technical editors, but it adds to the repertoire of skills editors must maintain, principally sales. They may find a sizable part of their work week absorbed by phone calls, networking luncheons, and job interviews, not all of them successful.

Here again, the answer is competence. Good, competent editors often prefer the contract system for its freedom, its higher rates, and its prestige.

## COMPETITION WITH OUR FRIEND, THE COMPUTER

Managers have always questioned the need for literate documents. Today, managers are increasingly wondering why editors cannot be replaced by machines, which are quicker and more accurate, and are daily becoming more clever.

The response need not be belabored. Computers cannot think. They can't make judgments or interpret. They cannot write. They can indeed spell. They can also search out and replace words; format, page-number, and index complete documents; and print perfect copies. But even on simple grammar tests, they flunk. "Style-checkers do best with rules that are mechanical," says Edmond Weiss (1990); "they do worst on problems of meaning and interpretation."

Unfortunately, too many editors let software do their work for them. They put their brains on automatic. They become keyboarders. What editors need to do is to exploit computers' marvelous capabilities for quick and accurate action, while reserving for themselves the capabilities that require intelligence and judgment.

Editing is cost-effective. Good editors can easily justify their salaries by the money they bring in with their effective sales brochures and new business proposals and the money they save with their lucid user manuals and copy-cutting, cost-reducing editing techniques.

## WHO'S IN CHARGE?

With the advent of desktop publishing, much document production has shifted away from the printing plant and into the office. With that shift, the traditional lines of responsibility have become blurred.

Traditionally, in industry the work of an editor was distinct from that of a subject expert, on one hand, and secretaries, proofreaders, artists, and printers, on the other. Now the subject experts have their own computers for originating their documents, and they may retain control of the files clear through the desktop publishing process.

Now, a computer file can become the site for collaborative activity. Documents can go from rough draft through multiple revisions and reviews to become camera-ready copy without anyone placing an editing mark on the manuscript.

One definite change is the growing political power of the people controlling the machines. In industry, document output can be controlled not by the proposal manager or the subject matter experts, but by the number of word processing machines available and the dedication of the operators. Even on major magazines, managing editors are finding that they have to fight for the right to make up the pages and select typefaces. The machines themselves have so much capability that their operators are able to take charge.

The answer, again, is competence. If the editor is unable or unwilling to make a wide range of decisions in writing, artwork, format, layout, typefaces, paper selection, and printing, these decisions fall to someone else—many times not to one who is trained for the task, but to a willing and eager keyboarder.

One of the big dangers to technical editors on the job today is that they may find themselves sitting in with the typists and reporting to a production manager who was formerly head of the steno pool. Such merged groups obviously tend to put the emphasis on the consistency of punctuation and capitalization rather than on the quality of the writing or the effectiveness of the message.

Once more, the solution to the problem is competence. A good editor can far outshine a keyboard operator in the quality of work produced.

The goal of editing is to reach the reader. No matter what trends emerge in the future, editors will always thrive if they have the skill to produce documents that the reader understands. And the key to this mutual understanding is a solid knowledge of language.

---

**LAYERS OF EDITING COMPETENCY**

A. Formatting. Establishing type styles, numbering, etc.

B. Catching typos. Following the style book. Policing capitalization, hyphenation, spacing, etc. Mini-editing.

C. Catching errors in grammar, usage, spelling, punctuation.

D. Improving the writing style. Decreasing wordiness. Applying the theme-rheme concept and the principles of Joseph Williams, Claire Cook, others.

E. Establishing unity and coherence, an extension of D. Fixing the order of sentences, paragraphs, and headings.

F. Finding the "Irish Bull." Applying common sense to problems of semantics, parallelism, zeugma, mixed metaphors, dangling elements, and sheer illogic.

G. Catching errors in content. Querying authors.

X. Editing artwork, A to G.

Y. Negotiating with authors. This is especially important in publishing books and scientific papers.

❖

A and B can be done with minimum skills (by typists, engineers, etc.). With practice, though, these skills become a specialty, and can be performed with great speed and accuracy.

C begins to require a knowledge of idiomatic English outside the rules.

D and E contain the principal body of editing knowledge. They require a basic ability to read accurately and translate clearly. They require the ability to write.

F requires only common sense and careful grammar, and thus is closely related to C. But it is often neglected.

G can require familiarity with the subject matter and related jargon. This comes quickly with experience.

X requires no formal art training, but rather a sense of audience and "Editing by Design," reinforced by experience.

Y requires some charm and persuasiveness. The most important quality, however, is manifest editing competence.

Each of these categories has many sublayers, and all of them overlap with the others.

---

# CHAPTER

## Editing for Content

As mentioned earlier, good editing is more than just a "quality assurance" that catches grammar gaffes and capitalization inconsistencies. That's style manual editing. Content editing not only helps catch technical errors, but also organizes the presentation and emphasizes the key points, making them not just readable, but appealing. Ideally, it focuses on the most pertinent data and makes the author's language sing. Some editors don't know the immense power of their profession.

Good editing can make the difference in a document between dismal failure and breathtaking, overwhelming success. If you as an editor can produce sales pitches that persuade customers, manuals that teach people, cautions/warnings that are really heeded, proposals that win contracts, and documents that are more appealing and less expensive, you will have no trouble justifying your own job and finding berths for all of your editor friends. Opportunities abound. Wordsmiths can be king.

"But that's not editing, that's rewriting," you say. Okay, but if it improves the copy, what you call the process is irrelevant (Hayakawa and Hayakawa 1990).

The Scribner approach—giving the responsibility for the writing to a Maxwell Perkins—is what we find among the publishers of books and periodicals.

Technical editors, too, need to assume more control of writing quality. They need to follow the proven techniques of professional industries, which, under the pressure of hourly deadlines, use incisive editors to help put out masses of well-written documents at low cost.

The technical editing profession needs to develop more content editors who can read the technical lingo. How can we pride ourselves on our accuracy when some editors don't even understand what the authors are saying? No wonder so much technical copy remains disorganized, diffuse, repetitious, wordy, and technically inaccurate. The inexperienced technical authors too seldom get real, magazine-type professional help in telling their stories.

## THE EDITING PROCESS

Editing technical writing is perhaps more demanding than editing other types of writing—books, newspapers, or magazines—because much technical writing is not done by professional writers.

A good editor looks for four things, in this order of importance:

1. Technical accuracy
2. Clarity
3. English correctness
4. English consistency

Good editors have a profound effect on technical accuracy. In the first place, they catch "gotchas." But more important is their ability to make the language—the *buts* and the *therefores*—conform to the actual facts.

However, the principal value of editors is their contribution to clarity. Briefly, clarity implies five things:

1. Logic
2. Organization
3. The use of natural language
4. Economy of words (See Chapter 3, "Cutting Copy.")
5. Emphasis

Clarity means readability. The object is to let readers read fast; when they can read quickly, they understand the material better and retain it. Certainly, they don't want to have to stop and figure things out.

Ordinarily, editors first check the overall organization. Sometimes they find a good statement that summarizes the problem and bring it up to the front. Then they divide the rest into convenient sections, perhaps using subheads. After that, they work on cutting down the wordiness and developing effective sentence and paragraph structure.

As an editor, you have to keep your brain turned on. You cannot edit just from a list of rules or pet peeves. You don't start with the rules and and hunt for violations. Instead, you read along until something "sounds funny," and then stop to fix it. As you go, your brain comes up with a way to convey the message more efficiently.

But when making changes in words or sentences, editors must be careful to consider the paragraph, or at times the entire page, to be sure the changes fit into the big picture.

## CONFORMING TO THE FACTS

As noted above, perhaps the most important duty of an editor is to make the language in a document conform to the actual facts. Editors have to do their best to make sure that the presentation is correct. This is the historic function of editors on newspapers and magazines, and even on technical journals.

On a technical proposal, the editor, as one of the few people who read inputs from all the technologies, has a responsibility to try to see that the write-ups jibe with one another. Again, as perhaps the last person to see the copy for a technical manual before printing, the editor has to check that no procedures have been left out. As the last pair of eyes to check the camera-ready copy on the annual report, the editor has to be doubly sure that something unthinkable has not happened to the company logo.

Among the many tasks of an editor—cutting copy, checking grammar and spelling, patrolling consistency, numbering the pages, or running a bindery check—no task is anywhere near as important as the job of maintaining technical correctness. And no talent is more greatly appreciated by authors, by supervisors, and by top management, than the ability to catch these all-too-frequent corporate "gotchas." So, ironically, even though editors without technical expertise cannot really be responsible for technical correctness, technical correctness is still their greatest responsibility.

## HOW CAN EDITORS JUDGE TECHNICAL ACCURACY?

But how are editors supposed to know what is "correct" in the field of medicine or computer science or structural dynamics? What if, when they change someone's copy, they themselves make a technical mistake?

Well, even if you are a conscientious editor, you will indeed goof now and then. But your editing errors will never get into the finished document; too many people will be looking over your shoulder.

And even your gaffes in themselves will turn out to be useful. They will open questions, leading to clearer explanations. Editors are thus used as reader surrogates, testing the prose as they go.

But when it gets right down to it, most of the written material in any technical field— thermodynamics, computer science, biology—is not very technical. The technical work goes on behind the scenes: tests, measurements, analyses, computer simulations. The actual presentation of the data is pretty simple, as it should be, because the reader is not always trained in that particular technology.

Often the reason that the copy sounds so complex is the convoluted sentence structure, the qualifications, the false starts.

Sometimes an editor can make some sense of hybrid "technicalese" simply by leading from her strength, her knowledge of sentence structure. If you know your English, you have a good start on understanding gobbledygook.

Logically, an editor can (1) find the subject, (2) put the verb next to it, and (3) follow with the complement, adverbs, or prepositional phrases to complete the clause or sentence.

Something to watch for is parallelism. Find the elements that are paired. Sometimes, the parallelism is faulty, and a simple correction makes it all come clear.

## LEARNING GOBBLEDYGOOK AS A SECOND LANGUAGE

Of course, you may not ever understand the sentence completely, because of what sometimes seems an impossible barrier of technical vocabulary.

However, even the technical vocabulary is often not so technical. In the first place, it may be full of generic gobbledygook jargon like *schema* or *paradigm*, which belongs to no one technology and which the editor can eliminate in order to understand the point.

It may also be loaded with technical jargon, which the editor can learn as she goes along. Ordinarily, the same technical terms appear time after time, because technical people who are absorbed in their subject have about the same vocabulary range as a drill sergeant. Even new words are not impossible to decipher; you can gather their mission from the context.

Once you gain experience with a subject, you begin to know it. You will never learn enough to be able to generate the data, but you can certainly check it to make it right.

Above all, editors must not join the "language police" (see Baron 1992). The whole idea of editing technical copy is to project mutual cooperation instead of confrontation. (See Chapter 13, "Getting Along with Authors.")

## LOGIC

Editors can also rely on many skills to find the clues that help them read technical copy, including, in particular, logic and a knowledge of language.

In the first place, editors know when the language is misused. They know about cause and effect. They know, by reading, when a step is left out or a "proof" remains unproven. The precepts of logic are not repealed when you enter the realm of biology.

Editors also know when the author is not sticking to the point, or is avoiding the main issues, or is speaking in biased terms. They know when she makes a false generalization. They learn to be wary of "therefores."

All of these problems are common in technical writing, and they are not hard for an editor to catch.

## LANGUAGE

Most of all, in reading technical copy, editors can bring to the table their knowledge of communicative language.

For instance, technical people often have trouble with the sequence of tenses. Is *if* in a dependent clause followed by *would* in the independent clause? Sometimes. (It's better just to try to stay away from the so-called "conditional tense" anyway, in favor of simple present and past.)

You do need to use the subjunctive, but most technical people have a good ear for it. It's only when they think about "grammar" that they do it wrong. "It is required that every mechanic learn . . . learns?"

One of the toughest writing problems for technical people is to talk about two things at once—to take a middle stance between two arguments. An editor can often sense the problem and is able to supply words to help out, like *on the other hand*, or *meanwhile*, or *nevertheless*, or *moreover*. Sometimes this vocabulary seems to be as bewildering to a technical person as *autocollimator* or *hemidemisemiquaver* to an editor.

The editor, as first reader, also has the responsibility to sniff out ambiguities, words or phrases that can mean more than one thing.

Good English is not just a matter of grammar. In fact, in technical writing, grammar is among the least of the problems. (With one major exception: parallelism. You would think that parallelism would appeal to structures engineers, but it doesn't. On the other hand, electronics people rarely make a parallelism error.)

A good editor can find plenty of opportunities to cut useless words (see Chapter 3, "Cutting Copy") and revise sentence structure. (See Chapter 6, "Sentences with Style.") But she can also find jumbled lists, disconnected writing, false starts, and clumsy writing not covered by Miss Thistlebottom.

## CATCHING "GOTCHAS"

We mentioned at the start of this chapter the accolades that accrue to editors who catch gotchas in an important document. The person who catches the customer's name misspelled on the cover of a proposal or who spots in the print shop on Sunday morning a "$6 million contract" with the "million" missing will get lasting credit.

Editors can set themselves up for such rewards. When you are editing, make a quick check of the right-hand digits of columns of figures. Make sure that a procedure really has seven steps, in the right order. Watch decimal points. And, especially, watch out for exaggerated claims.

Technical people are smart, but they are sometimes sloppy about details that don't challenge their minds. They get wrapped up in listening to the music of their own prose and commit a surprising number of elementary errors.

As a nontechnical type, you might have an advantage. You *need* all seven steps to understand the problem. You *can't understand* why a coil is installed on the left in the text and on the right in the figure. You have to ask questions, and those very questions help clear up the problem and make the explanation simpler, and more accurate, for the next reader.

If you can catch their mistakes, the technical people may say, "I didn't know you knew so much about thermodynamics!" And they will be sure to let your eyes see the copy next time. In fact, it may be the engineering manager who makes that request. "Do you mind?" he will ask. "I don't have the time today to read it myself."

This is one of the ironic things that sometimes happens in technical writing. The technical people get busy writing for posterity, thus leaving the rhetoric majors to look for the technical mistakes, each doing the job for which they are least well equipped.

## TIME

Just how much time does all this extra checking take? At first, quite a bit. And you can't take all the time in the world. The reports are big, and they have rigid deadlines. You do have to work fast. (See Chapter 12 on working under tight deadlines.)

But you will keep getting faster. You'll learn the terminology quickly, get to know the people, and get used to what you need to check. You will take more time on the important material, less time on the routine. Soon you will be able to keep up with the output of a group, then a larger unit, and then a whole floor of people.

You can begin to see the advantages for a company of using editors rather than so many individual technical writers. In the old days, a technical writer would interview a subject expert (SE) and go off to write the section. Then the SE would edit the writer, perhaps several times, until she got it right. Thus, the writer, instead of handling a whole floor of people, was attached almost full time to one individual.

## THE PROCESS OF CONTENT EDITING

In summary, here are some quick suggestions about content editing, which each individual should chew carefully before swallowing. Editing styles vary widely.

1. Start with what you know. Use your high school training to catch errors in grammar and style. The stylebook still plays a part in "content editing."
2. Begin cleaning out the structure. As a writer, you are an expert on structure and, fortunately for you, that's where you'll find the most confusion in technical material. Break the sentences into clauses and experiment by putting the main point of each clause at the end, in the stress position. Run the words through your brain, asking yourself, "How would I say this face-to-face?"
3. As you recombine the clauses back into sentences, cut out the repetition and general clutter. Supply missing parallelism.
4. Use the main point at the end of each sentence to start the next sentence. Notice now that the message, while still fuzzy, begins to at least make a coherent chain.
5. Add a framework to orient the reader in the form of introductory phrases and other means of continuity and, above all, a summary or a statement of the problem.
6. Collar the busy author assertively to confirm that what you are doing is technically accurate. Listen, and make the changes.
7. As you go, scrutinize the words. In a matter of days, you can indeed begin to recognize the vocabulary. But avoid changing it. Technical words are editors' literary landmines.
8. Then, as you gain confidence, work on catching careless technical gotchas, which, as mentioned, is the editing that authors most appreciate.
9. Eventually, help the author improve her pitch by suggesting new angles, artwork, persuasive adjectives.

You'll never learn the technical content well enough to run the tests yourself. But almost from the beginning you will be able to understand the author's intended message and help her to communicate it to her readers.

## MORE IS NOT BETTER

You will note that as your edited copy becomes clearer, it often becomes shorter (or, if you prefer, vice versa). This is a massive benefit for the company, far greater than policing hyphens. Most technical copy is too voluminous.

In proposals, editorial copy-cutting helps authors meet their limits without dropping information they prize. Soon they will be saying appreciatively to you, in their native engineeringese, "You cut things out without cutting things out." Your skill can become invaluable.

Proposal experts today are beginning to realize that sections should not be written to page limits, but rather edited down to them. (See Appendix B, "Editing Technical Proposals.") The text is then tighter. This copy-cutting is one of the greatest growing opportunities for professional editors.

In manuals, shortening the copy as you organize it makes instructions more accessible. (See Appendix A, "Editing Technical Manuals.") It also cuts production costs and saves on desk and storage space, especially in aircraft crew stations. Good editing can add similar efficiencies to letters, bulletins, position papers, procedures, handbooks, journal articles, and all the rest. Once you begin to provide your company such tangible benefits, you can ask for status.

When you ask some editors about trying content editing, one of their excuses is, "The authors won't let me." But content editing does indeed make sense to engineers, proposal managers, computer systems engineers, and even accountants. They know that their writing needs more organization and impact to bring out their technical ideas.

## EDITING ON SCREEN

The computer has caused many editors to work differently. Subject experts may do their own typing, and editors (less frequently) may edit on screen. Can an editor still make her voice heard? (See Chapter 13, "Getting Along with Authors.")

There is no reason why not. It depends, however, almost entirely on the trust and the respect the editor commands.

## THE REWARDS OF CONTENT EDITING

Content editing does have its rewards. A company can afford to pay a content editor more than a stylebook editor because the work is more valuable.

But, more than that, content editing is far more interesting. Instead of checking figure numbers, or tracking down capitalization, you are learning about the project itself and are much more closely involved in its presentation. You can indeed become vitally interested in a rocket launch, or a computerized training program, or artificial intelligence, or fuzzy logic, or virtual reality.

True, not all editing is exciting. But when you are learning about things on the frontier of science, and are trying to think of ways to make them live in the minds of a wide variety of readers, you begin to feel that you are part of something important and useful.

## EXAMPLES OF CONTENT EDITING

If a person printing on one interface cancels a print job (or it is otherwise "abnormally terminated" such as by a power failure), the printer will wait five minutes before accepting data from another interface.

If a job on one interface is terminated abnormally, the printer will wait five minutes before accepting a job on another interface.

❖

Most software applications allow you to choose printing instructions from a menu or enter printing instructions (escape sequences) directly in your file. However, this method of controlling your printer requires you to learn printer commands.

Most software allows you to choose printing instructions from a menu, or, if you know the printing commands, to insert them directly.

❖

As you select paper for your XYZ printer, be sure to choose only paper in the 16- to 24-lb range. Colored photocopy, bond, and letterhead paper, or preprinted forms that fall within this range may be used in the printer.

Your XYZ printer can use plain bond, letterhead, or preprinted forms, in all colors. Just be sure your paper is 16 to 24 lb.

❖

The Ready button, when pressed, will either turn the printer on (Ready light is on and the printer is ready), or turn the printer off (Ready light is off and printer will not function).

The Ready button, when pressed, will light and turn the printer on. Pressed again, it will turn the printer off.

❖

WARNING: This equipment generates, uses, and can radiate radio frequency energy and, if not installed in accordance with the instructions manual, may cause interference to radio communications.

WARNING: This equipment generates RF energy and if not installed according to the manual can cause radio interference.

❖

As the carriage moves across the platen, a light emitting diode and a light sensor on the carriage detect movement as they pass over a stationary encoder strip.

The carriage contains a light emitting diode and a sensor. As it passes over an encoder strip on the platen, it senses movement.

# CHAPTER

# 3

## Cutting Copy

In professional publications, space is extremely valuable. The publishing process costs money, and costs are figured right down to the printed line. So far, the technical writing business is much more casual. The major exception is on proposals, where page limits are rigidly enforced and every author is on a stringent diet of wordage. The ability to cut out words from proposals without cutting out meaning becomes extremely valuable.

The day is coming, too, when authors of software manuals will be asked to cut wordage, much to the benefit of the user.

The chief fault in most technical writing is not grammar; it is wordiness. This is a well-kept secret in publications offices, which may be paid by the page. But someday, management will find out that manuals don't have to be so big, and editors will suddenly achieve greatness.

A good editor wields a double-edged sword. By cutting copy drastically, she can cut costs and, at the same time, make the copy much more understandable (Holtz 1986).

"Words are like trees, and where they most abound, Much fruit of sense beneath is seldom found."
—Alexander Pope

## FIXING WORDY WRITING

Some editors, rightly concerned with preserving the feelings of the authors, simply do not realize how bad technical writing can get. Here's one example:

```
Timely production and delivery of
high-quality concise, accurate docu-
mentation which meets all customer
requrements is vital in assuring that
performance of their mission can be
achieved by having the necessary re-
ports and documents available when
needed and by having all technical
information thoroughly documented.
```

Something in all this is simply not needed.
Note in the following sentence what can be excised.

```
This is because there may be numer-
ous satisfactory approaches to solve
```

~~an engineering problem or to develop a computer system and~~
changes may be desired after the report ~~or specification~~ is
already on paper.

Here's another actual example of wordy writing, modified slightly to protect the
perpetrators.

Our plan includes separation of application software from
physical data access and storage considerations so as to
enable the installation and production use of software
developments produced by the Integrated Sheet Metal Center
(ISMC) and the Advanced Machining System (AMS) and application software produced by other companies or outside software houses as it becomes available and as we extend our
implementations throughout the factory.

## THE PROCESS FOR CUTTING COPY

How do you attack such overblown sentences? Here are a few suggestions that might
apply:

1.  Find the true subject and true verb.
2.  Eliminate unneeded doublets.
3.  Eliminate smothered verbs ("tion" words).
4.  Eliminate repetition.
5.  Decide what else is not needed.
6.  Find a punch word for the end.

Of course, poor writing takes many forms. Here's an
example that involves faulty structure:

Our plan includes modularity of system
design so as to provide standardized gateways of communications between levels of
control, standard interfaces with various
classes of shop floor devices, and the
ability to enable production implementation of new techological data processing
improvements as they become available in
the areas of network communication, terminal interfaces, and data management.

➕

**Pleonasm is to technical
prose as neoplasm is
to living tissue: always
debilitating and
often fatal.**

This is a problem in parallelism, the technical term being "apples and oranges." You
see that *modularity* provides three things: *gateways*, *interfaces*, and *ability*, but they
are not parallel. Here's one possible solution:

Our plan includes modular design that will standarize the
communication between levels of control and the interfaces
between shop floor devices and will produce better hardware
for networks and terminals and for data management.

Now the *three* things have become *two* parallel actions (*standardize* and *produce*),
one of which contains *two* parallel items (*communication* and *interfaces*.) Once you
fix that, the rest is easy.

You see the importance of knowing structure. This is the technology of English, applied to engineering.

## OTHER FAULTS

There are an infinite number of faults in technical copy, most of which defy any classification and appear together in massive combinations. However, here are a few things to watch for. These categories follow closely the ideas of Joseph Williams in *Style: Ten Lessons in Clarity & Grace,* using technical examples with problems italicized:

**Belaboring the obvious**

> *There are primarily two methods of presenting information that can utilize visual aids: expository writing and oral communication.*

**Sounding pompous**

> *Affix signature of approval on 502A and forward to the cognizant management administrators.* . . .

**Over qualifying**

> Tables are used to present numerical *and tabulated* data that would be difficult to *simulate and* interpret *had it been written within the* text.

**Using phrases for words**

> The procedures for *accomplishment of* the annual training survey have some operational weaknesses. . . . *Implementation of* the new system should improve the annual needs survey . . .

**Being redundant**

> *The planned approaches for definition of* the new *and/or modified* operating requirements *identified above* are *essentially as* outlined above.

**Hedging**

> These varieties *tend to* ripen *relatively* quickly after picking and *have a marked tendency to* break down at the core.

**Talking about the report instead of the topic**

> *The purpose of this report is to* introduce an infrared search and track model . . .
>
> We have recently developed an infrared search and track model . . .

**Burying the topic**

> *It is anticipated that* early next year an automated system will be available . . .

These sentences are much shorter than most of those in technical copy. Also most bad sentences will have not just one of these faults, but rather combinations, attached in imposing towers of obfuscation. Thus, one sentence may fit many categories.

Note especially that most redundancies do not occur at the sentence level; they are found largely in the paragraph and the section.

So, in sum, your best guide to cutting copy is simply your common sense. Don't try to follow any rules too rigidly. Just, for instance, be aware that sometimes you actually need to hedge or even be a little redundant.

## ADDING IN ORDER TO SUBTRACT

Many times, instead of omitting words, editors must *build* a solution from ground zero. Take our previous example:

```
Timely production and delivery of high-quality concise,
accurate documentation which meets all customer requrements
is vital in assuring that performance of their mission can
be achieved by having the necessary reports and documents
available when needed and by having all technical informa-
tion thoroughly documented.
```

This is a basket case. The editor simply needs to start over. Here's how she might do it.

1.  Find the true subject, true verb, true object. (In severe cases, these have to be invented.)

    ```
    Users need documents.
    ```

2.  Add framework (eliminating passive voice and smothered verbs)

    ```
    To be sure they can perform their mission, users need docu-
    ments.
    ```

3.  Add pertinent adjectives.

    ```
    To be sure they can perform their mission, users need docu-
    ments that are timely, accurate, concise, and complete.
    ```

Of course, the editor does this quickly, by using the marvelous capability of the human brain. He might say, "How would I say this if the customer is going out the door?"

(You will find more details on editing sentences in Chapter 6, "Sentences with Style.")

This kind of sentence is not unusual; such heavy editing is often needed, especially in proposals, where page limits apply and the writing is anonymous. In the case of professional papers, where space and sales impact are less important than the author's self-respect, editing must be much less severe.

## COLLABORATION WITH THE AUTHOR

But what about the feelings of the author?

Technical men and women are practical, logical people and seldom object to having their thoughts brought out more succinctly. This is especially so if they are under a page limit, as in a proposal, or have been asked to write a short set of instructions that is "really clear."

All people are super-sensitive about their writing, of course, so editors need to be cautious. The best approach is to show, like a good teacher, that you are always on the author's side. Chapter 13 offers some tips on dealing with authors.

By the way, veteran editors say that pride of authorship runs highest among professional writers, English teachers, and other editors.

## DEADWOOD GULCH

The path to clarity is often overgrown with "deadwood." This verbal underbrush can be chopped out, resulting in a more precise presentation of facts. For instance, when you read that "a system description will be prepared to describe an instrumentation system," something is unnecessary. Take your pick of what to cut.

In the copy-chopping process, the editor takes the copy apart and throws away the deadwood. Ironically, this deadwood tends to be the same, no matter what the subject.

> **Deadwood expressions**
> for the purpose of
> in the case of
> in the area of
> in the field of
> in connection with
> on the part of
> through the use of
> in conditions of
> as far as _____ is
>   concerned

The deadwood expressions shown in the boxed list are not "wrong," but often they can be cleared out and replaced with a simple *for, by,* or *with.*

Other examples are:

```
due to the fact that = since, because

at this point in time = now

despite the fact that = although
```

## DOUBLETS

One of the easiest ways to cut copy is to eliminate "doublets," like *prepare and submit,* or *separately and supplementally.* Joseph Williams claims in *Style: Ten Lessons in Clarity and Grace* (1994) that the custom began in English because ours was a hybrid language, stemming from both Latin and Germanic roots, and so people got into the habit of trying to make themselves clear by using words from both stems (*manual* and *handbook*).

Nowadays we find we don't need both; we sound too pretentious. So editors make copy clearer by choosing one of them to chop: "Methods and procedures have been devised and developed to establish and maintain . . ." That sounds too military; it is clearer to simply write, "We have developed procedures to establish . . ."

Look for doublets in scientific reports, book reviews, campus memos, annual reports, junk mail, sales brochures, government pamphlets . . . anyplace where bad writing abounds.

## REDUNDANT MODIFIERS

Perhaps when striving for emphasis, authors sometimes employ the same thought twice: *final* authority, *basic* fundamentals, *necessary* prerequisite, *significant* meaning, *meaningful* significance. Ironically, you can see that we are generally more emphatic when we simply say *authority*, or *significance*.

Moreover, people sometimes use "backup" words. These weak creatures fit almost anywhere; you will find them attached as follows: *currently* anticipated, *current* status, *necessary* qualifications, *existing* conditions, *appropriate* measures, *pertinent* or *cognizant* management, *specific* requirements, *representative* achievements.

Sometimes an editor cannot remove these parasites because it simply sounds better to leave them in. Or the words may add something in context, particularly in contrast: *existing* conditions vs. those of *yesterday*.

Similarly, redundancy is frequently used in connection with acronyms, as in *SALT talks*, the *AIDS syndrome*, the *Amoco Company*. An editor will retain redundancy when it makes meaning clearer or it sounds better. You can't always go by rules. You have to keep your brain turned on.

> **Redundant phrases:** because of *the fact that,* whether *or not*
> **Redundant category words:** large *in size,* green *in color,* rumpled *in appearance*
> **Redundant modifiers:** *free* gift, *solid* brick wall, *past* history
> **Weak qualifiers:** *fairly* good, *somewhat* complex
> **Oxymorons:** *rather* unique, *almost* equal, *more* complete
> **Subject buriers:** *As far* as X *is concerned, It has been observed that, In regard to*

## SMOTHERED VERBS

One of the greatest redundancies in nonprofessional technical writing is the smothered verb. It is often revealed by a "-tion word," or a verb transformed into a noun and sometimes called a "nominalization," as in:

```
Evaporation of the liquid takes place.
```

Most writers prefer to say:

```
The liquid evaporates.
```

The true verb in both sentences is *evaporates*, but in the first sentence, the nominalization "smothers" the verb, which is replaced by a flabbier generic verb, i.e., *takes place*.

Here are other examples:

```
Extrapolation of system performance cannot be made readily
to the 2000 time period. ⇒ System performance cannot be
extrapolated to 2000.
```

```
Maximum use of this body of knowledge will be made, includ-
ing adaption of existing systems where practical. ⇒ XYZCO
will use this knowledge fully, adapting systems when prac-
tical.

Analyses and tests will aid in definition of the system. ⇒
Analyses and tests will help define the system.
```

A good editor will also watch for smothered verbs in nominalizations ending in
*-sion, -ment*, and even *-ing*.

```
Revisions  of  the  trajectory  profiles  will  be  made
periodically. ⇒ Trajectory profiles will be revised peri-
odically.

To provide for the accomplishment of (b), effort will be
applied as outlined above.  ⇒  To accomplish (b), effort
will be applied as outlined above.

A test plan will be defined for the obtaining of the data.
⇒ A test plan will be defined to obtain the data.
```

In general, the editor will prefer "finite" verbs, or root stems that can be declined
(obtain, obtains, obtained).

```
We will be finishing our study with measurements on films
having resistance to heat. ⇒ To finish our study, we will
measure films that resist heat.

For adjustment of the tuner, a theory of operation for
these devices must be developed. ⇒ To adjust the tuner, we
must first develop a theory about how it operates.
```

One important caveat: We should not outlaw all nominalizations. We need them as
nouns. We question here only their use as smothered verbs.

## REDUNDANCY IN THOUGHT

Up to this point, we have concentrated on eliminating redundancy in word usage. But
an editor can accomplish even more if he concentrates on redundancies in thought.
    Too often, authors belabor the obvious, as in:

```
Trainers are equipment capable of performing one or more
specific operating and/or maintenance functions by use of
simulated means and/or actual system assemblies or parts.
```

This was an actual sentence in a training report. It reduces to:

```
Trainers are assemblies or parts that can simulate operat-
ing or maintenance functions.
```

Here's another, from the advance sheet on a traveling huckster who should
know better:

```
The field of technical writing is a significant and growing
one. This new meeting will discuss the problems of writing
technical manuals. Among the topics to be discussed are
those of writing styles and their use in conjunction with
technical manuals. Special considerations involved in pre-
senting technical material in order to make it interesting
and useful will be considered. Another important area of
discussion will be indexing, editing, and auditing techni-
cal manuals. Considerable time will be devoted to the best
ways in which charts, exhibits, and illustrations can be
used for maximum effectiveness.
```

This becomes:

```
Technical writing is a growing field. At this meeting we
will discuss how to write technical material that is inter-
esting and useful. We will also show how to edit, index,
and audit technical manuals and how to use illustrations,
charts, and other exhibits for maximum effectiveness.
```

## A FIRM NOTE OF CAUTION

Beginning editors can readily see the advantages of chopping copy to save space. But another object of editing is to make copy more understandable.

Your editing short cuts must therefore be both technically correct and acceptable to human readers. Just as certain ultra-rigid grammatical rules must be squelched in order to prevent expressions like "It's I" or "Whom is he kidding?", an editor cannot always use the shortest path, or his copy will sound funny. You can sometimes prove this fact by looking at copy that is edited by an overzealous technical person.

Idiom and clarity always take preference over brevity. Therefore, it is possible to make a very few "rules" for inserting words and making copy longer.

1. Reject telegraphic, or headline, style. Use plenty of *the*'s, as discussed in Chapter 5, "Words."
2. Do not remove the relative pronoun *that*. In a short sentence, such as "I know that the solution is correct," *that* can safely be omitted, but in long ones with many embedded clauses, the pronoun offers a valuable signpost for the reader.
3. Be careful about removing *in order to*. Consider the sentence "The guards are required in order to let the women sleep." This is an extreme example, but *in order to* often makes a sentence clearer and more idiomatic. Sometimes, if you remove it, it should be replaced by a comma: "I take my own car, to save time."
4. There are many cases in long sentences where insertion of structure helps the reader recall where he is. Sometimes it is an infinitive "to," as in "I come here to swim, to play, and to have fun." Other times it is a "have" or a "will."
5. There are "rules" against starting sentences with expletives, such as *there is* or *it is*. These little words do take space, but sometimes they are needed to give a key word emphasis at the end of the sentence. (See Chapter 6, "Sentences with Style.") "It was the best of times, it was the worst of times. . . ."

6.  You will often want to insert words to remove ambiguity. If you say "Publishing costs money," that's a broader concept than saying "The publishing process costs money." Inserting an extra word makes the statement more precise. Technical people often thank editors for inserting words to make their meanings clearer. And also for inserting an occasional adjective to sharpen a concept.

For clarity, you may occasionally need to insert words that are somehow missing. You read:

```
The company's strategy of building or buying capacity when
one approach better serves our company worked well last
year.
```

Instead, try this:

```
The company's flexible strategy of either building or buy-
ing capacity, whichever better served our needs, worked
well last year.
```

Here's another example:

```
The journey receives no accolades. But the destination
does.
```

The author was striving for fine writing, but he could have influenced the reader more powerfully had he said, ". . . arrival at the destination. . . ."

## OTHER EDITING PLOYS

Of course, there is more to editing than adding or subtracting words. As you go, you're likely to find **disconnected writing**:

```
The vitality of our service area is directly tied to your
company's future success. Low energy prices, reliable en-
ergy supplies, and quality customer and community service
are all important in developing the local economy. When
combined, these factors will determine the long-term fu-
ture success of your Company.
```

Such loose bundles of verbiage won't ever survive the post office. Tie the message together like this:

```
The future success of your company is tied to the vitality
of our service area. We propose to contribute to the area's
economy by providing reliable energy and quality service at
low prices, while participating in the community.
```

The fun really starts when you begin to block those **over-vivid metaphors**:

```
This unparalleled geographic scope is harnessed to an un-
matched ability to handle large, complex transactions.
```

Or:

> The choices of the future still will be geared toward managing for the long term and anticipating change in our business environment, but with each challenge, stronger organization will ensue.

The author took the latter excursion to explain a corporate shakeup, and you can hear the gears grinding all the way, even though he double-clutched.

Here's another one:

> According to stereotype, the successful banker and his satisfied customer routinely met on the first tee. No more. Today, they're more likely to team up on the cutting edge, where the astute banker creates new products and services to meet changing market needs.

Those golf course mowers have more room than one would think.

Naturally, you will want to chomp down on **misleading sentence structure**:

> Since 1970, 16 crocodile nests here have produced 124 known hatchlings that were marked and released to monitor this endangered species.

While the hatchlings are monitoring the endangered species, who's keeping an eye out for those crocodiles?

Even a nontechnical reader can discover **technical lapses**:

> Combined-cycle units are highly efficient because they join a combustion turbine—operating like a jet engine—with a heat recovery system to produce steam for further electric generation, making the same energy do double duty.

While also repealing the laws of thermodynamics? Better would be something like this:

> Combined-cycle units are highly efficient because they re-cover waste heat from the gas-fired combustion turbine generator and use it to produce steam for . . .

Note that for this application the jet engine is not as good an analogy as the homely automobile heater.

Also look for self-conscious **false starts**:

> It's an elusive task to bring to life in an annual report just what it is a financial services company does.

Nearly always you find, farther along, a more businesslike beginning, like *"This year . . ."*

In all cases, the editor's job is to help the reader read quickly, with clear under-standing and without any interruptions. Cutting and rearranging copy are valuable in helping the reader achieve this goal.

# CHAPTER

## Document Organization

Editors are confirmed nitpickers. They are concerned with commas and capital letters and spelling and grammar and type fonts and punctuation and line spacing and consistency. This "microediting" is indeed part of the editing job.

But a more important and difficult editing function is to straighten out the overall organization of a document, sometimes called "macroediting." Like a good editor of films, an editor of technical documents must introduce the subject, show its interest, and sustain that interest through a logical, orderly sequence that is easy to follow and understand, while she blends the whole thing together with continuity.

Macroediting can work miracles in connecting authors with their audiences. Good editors have the rare ability to take disparate elements and tie them together into a cogent message.

### FINDING THE STORY

The editor's first job is to find the story the author wants to tell and help him tell it so the reader will respond. The editor needs to ask: What is the overall problem? What does the user need? Why is the message relevant? What is the story?

Unfortunately, too many technical documents don't have a story. Joseph Williams points out in seminars that, quite often, a paper offers no problem. And without a problem, it's hard to develop a solution. This means that, for the editor, the main problem is to find the problem.

Similarly, many documents tell the wrong story. A simple example is the engineer who tries to *define* systems engineering (most often unsuccessfully) instead of *using* systems engineering to solve an engineering puzzle. Or an electronics engineer may describe the *background* of artificial intelligence rather than its *potential*. Such reports do not address the right problem.

"It's often hard to decompose problems," says Williams. How right he is. The task of editors, as readers' surrogates, is to help the author address the readers' questions. This means editors must often work backwards to find the missing problem, as in a complex game of TV Jeopardy!

Once the problem is determined, editors often have to ferret out detail. They have to query the author. What specific steps will be taken to solve that problem? What decisions must be made, and how will each of these decisions affect the solution? What are the technical tradeoffs, and how will these tradeoffs be weighed? These are questions that the reader is going to ask, and the editor can be the reader's surrogate.

The process just described is admittedly advanced editing, which is beyond the ken of many editors but not always beyond their abilities. It's where the excitement lies in the profession. It's the type of editing often demanded of book editors, or editors of newspapers and magazines.

It's not as difficult as it might seem, but it's all part of "macroediting," which addresses the big picture rather than just line spacing and semicolons.

## INDUCTIVE AND DEDUCTIVE STRUCTURE

One of the editor's most important tasks in macroediting is ensuring that the structure of a document is logical and helpful to the reader. Scientists are proud of their analytical, inductive, building-block approach, but insiders reveal that scientific research seldom works that way. (See, for example, biologist Sir Peter Medawar's article "Is the Scientific Paper Fraudulent? Yes; It Misrepresents Scientific Thought.") Researchers commonly postulate a theory and then proceed desperately to throw everything

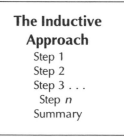

**The Inductive
Approach**
Step 1
Step 2
Step 3 . . .
Step $n$
Summary

they can find at the problem to make the hypothesis come true. ("It's not working. Let's try tungsten!")

There's nothing wrong with this procedure; it's standard practice. But you do have to stretch a point to call it a building-block approach.

Many technical authors write in this same trial-and- error mode. They flit from topic to topic as though they were building nothing more sturdy than a bird's nest, inserting here and there little twigs of thought. Then, to organize their opus, they number the subsections, making sure that Section 2.3.2 follows Section 2.3.1.

That's where they need good macro editing, with emphasis on structure, organization, logic, and paragraphing.

There is a major dilemma, though, about organizational structure.

Most engineers prefer the building-block approach to preparing documents. They gather the facts, one by one, and assemble them into a finished structure.

For all its faults as a research method, this is still an impeccable way to build a building, or design an airplane, or bake a cake. It's an especially good way to test circuits; technicians test each component and then put them together into subsystems and methodically test each subsystem. In testing, there is no better way.

This inductive approach frequently carries over into engineering writing. In a planning meeting for a document, someone will almost always suggest, "Let's go chronologically."

But in most technical reports, chronological order may be the worst way to go. The reason is that chronological order places the new news—the results, the most important part—at the very end. In technical documents, especially new-business proposals, this is deadly.

Therefore the editor must help the author to avoid starts like:

| **The Deductive Approach** |
| --- |
| Summary |
| Details, Subsystem 1 |
| Details, Subsystem 2 |
| Details, Subsystem 3 . . . $n$ |

```
The first function that Quality Assurance
performs is receiving inspection . . .

Back in 1911, in a barn at the edge of a
wheat field . . .

Structures people have been working with
titanium since 1950 . . .
```

Instead, the editor needs to promote starts that tell the story right away:

```
Scientists at XYZ believe that they have opened an important
window to the universe with the development of . . .

Metal matrix composites are rapidly supplanting titanium for
high temperature structural applications on . . .
```

Of course, chronological order does have its place. It's absolutely the best way to write a history and most biographies. Also, it's a good organizational structure for process specifications or for instructional manuals, where, obviously, Step 1 must precede Step 2 and Step 2 must precede Step 3, in strict order (as discussed in Appendix A "Editing Technical Manuals").

But in most technical writing, the author needs to get to the meat first. That's where the reader is still reading!

Henrietta Tichy, in *Effective Writing for Engineers, Managers, Scientists* (1988), says it this way: "A reader usually wishes to know not what has been reported in the literature during the last 150 years, but what has not been reported."

For a discussion on inductive and deductive, see Winterowd (1975) and many others.

In the engineering memo shown in Example 4.1, the writer evidently wanted his manager to follow him through all the twists and turns of the project. The information that answers the manager's probable questions—does it work and what does it cost?—takes some getting to.

Burke needed an editor who was thinking about Polston's needs, interests, and available time. That editor would probably have produced a memo like the one shown in Example 4.2.

To: C. R. Polston, Operations Manager

From: R. S. Burke, Project Engineer

Subject: Report on Portable Production Test
   Facilities for Gas Wells

Date: June 1, 1994

A portable skid-mounted test tank complete with an oil-gas separator was constructed to measure flow rates of gas, liquid, and liquid-gas mixtures from drill stem tests and production wells. These operations are remote and lack both labor and services. It was necessary to design a simple, functional, and self-contained unit. Satisfactory test results were the goal of the design.

The types of wells that would be tested with this unit were originally anticipated to be gas wells. The major problem would be one of freezing and hydrate formation in the gas due to 0° F climatic temperatures and the cooling effect of expanding gas caused by a pressure decrease. The use of an indirect fired heater to heat the gas would add another separate package to the moves between locations. A unit was designed utilizing a critical flow prover to measure the gas flow and pressure the system. The pressure drop and gas expansion would occur at the end of the gas flare line.

High gas-oil ratio wells were first anticipated. The unit was equipped with a dump valve. This was used successfully in other gas fields. This dump valve is "snap-acting" in design. This precludes fluid cutting of the valve seat or leakage at low liquid rates of flow and is limited to a ¼" orifice. This size valve is too small for flow rates of 1,000 B/D at only 200 psi well pressures. A manual bypass throttling arrangement was installed to accommodate high (1,000 B/D) liquid flow rates. Use of a floatless level controller in place of the dump valve is now being investigated.

The cost of this unit was approximately $27,000 and has been satisfactory in measuring the (1) produced fluid recovered in drill stem tests to establish whether a drilling well is commercial, (2) treating fluids recovered used to complete the wells such as acid, fracing oil, etc., and (3) produced fluid recovered on short duration production tests after completion of the well to furnish data for the type of surface facilities required.

ENGINEER'S MEMO USING INDUCTIVE APPROACH.

**EXAMPLE 4.1**

## DEVELOPING THE START

Many times the editor needs to reach down into the composition and pluck out the message, in a specific single sentence, putting it at the start. The reader will be grateful.

Sooner or later, the author will write that sentence that says it all: the "peg" on which his entire composition hangs. It's up to the editor to find it, whether on page 3 or page 10, and bring it up front as in Example 4.2.

An editor can also help make that peg more specific by inserting numbers, details, or facts.

To: C. R. Polston, Operations Manager

From: R. S. Burke, Project Engineer

Subject: Portable Unit for Testing Exploratory Wells

Date: June 24, 1994

A self-contained portable unit was constructed, at a cost of $27,000, for measuring flow rates of gas, liquid, and liquid-gas mixtures from drill stem and production tests at remote exploratory wells. The unit has worked satisfactorily. It measures (1) produced fluid recovered in drill stem tests for determining whether a drilling well is commercial, (2) recovered treating fluids (used to complete the wells) such as acid, fracing oil, etc., and (3) produced fluid recovered on short production tests for determining surface-facility requirements.

The test unit had to be portable and simple. Test sites are remote, and labor and outside services are not readily available.

The unit, originally designed to be used primarily with gas wells, was designed for 2,000 psi working pressure. Thus a chief design consideration was to avoid freezing and gas hydrate formation, which result from low outdoor winter temperatures and the cooling effects produced when gas pressure drops rapidly.

To meet these design considerations, particularly the avoidance of gas hydrate formation, gas is measured with a critical flow prover, which allows all the gas-pressure drop to be taken at the end of the flare line. The alternative choice of an indirect-fired gas heater was discarded because adding another bulky unit would make transportation more difficult.

For wells with high gas-oil ratios, the unit was equipped with a dump valve used successfully in other gas fields. The dump valve is "snap-acting" to preclude fluid cutting of the valve seat or leakage at low flow rates, but its orifice size is limited to 1/4". Although satisfactory for the high gas-oil ratio wells, this valve is too small for liquid-flow rates of 1,000 barrels per day at around 200-psi well pressure. Therefore, a manual bypass throttling valve was installed to accommodate these high flow rates. To replace the dump valve, we are investigating a floatless liquid-level controller.

ENGINEER'S MEMO EDITED FOR MANAGER'S NEEDS.

**EXAMPLE 4.2**

"Suppose you are reporting results of a survey on use of aluminum in automobiles," says Norman Shidle in *Clear Writing Makes Easy Reading* (1951). "Your peg might be: 'Less aluminum will be used in automobiles next year than in any recent year.' Not 'Data on prospects for use of aluminum in automobiles next year. . . .' "

Start with a statement of the problem or a solution, directed to the proper audience. As soon as an author has that in mind, he can begin his outline!

## BAD STARTS

An editor should knock out starts like "This manual will describe. . . ." Especially, do not allow a start such as "Chapter 1 contains . . . , Chapter 2 contains. . . ." That brands the author as being more interested in his book than in the product. If the author feels compelled to talk about his own work, make him put it in the preface.

Likewise, avoid starting with rhetorical questions. They are a convoluted way of introducing straight facts. And especially avoid starting with a quotation or a definition. In addition to being dull, these devices mark the author as not having much exciting to say and, instead, trying to be literary.

Find the peg that will interest the reader, said in 20 to 30 words. It will launch your reader into the best of all possible beginnings.

## PLANNING THE ORGANIZATION

There are many ways to organize a report. A few examples are shown in the text box (Ways to Organize). These are by no means all of the ways to organize; the point is that the editor needs to look beyond chronological order.

Most of the time, organizing technical reports is easy: the author simply follows what other authors did last year. Perhaps this is not a bad idea.

At any rate, it's a mistake for writers to be arty for the sake of being different. Certainly, change from last year's routine is good, but it needs to be supported by firm, independent reasons. In fact, as editors peruse the "praiseworthy efforts" of some young, unlettered engineers, they may come to the reluctant conclusion that one of the principal jobs of an editor is to stomp out errant "creativity."

> **The Peg**
>
> **A Statement**
> "XYZ has developed an inexpensive new PC software that . . ."
>
> **A Problem**
> "New, noninvasive methods are needed to . . ."
>
> **A Statement and a Problem**
> "IBM's new MacPac software may solve the problem of . . ."
>
> **A Problem and a Statement**
> "To meet a growing demand, XYZ plans . . ."
>
> **A Hypothesis**
> "An obscure tree fungus could affect . . ."
>
> **A Forecast**
> "By the year 2020, industry will face a serious shortage of . . ."

## ALPHABETICAL ORGANIZATION

Some lazy manual writers ignore the organization problem entirely by approaching topics alphabetically, as in an encyclopedia. But this approach has many disadvantages.

1. It's poor for instruction. It describes *Pop-up screen elements* ahead of *Screen elements*, with potential chaos.
2. It takes topics out of their natural associations. *Ascenders* and *Descenders* each show up separately, and a long way from *Typefaces* or *Fonts*.
3. It requires frequent cross-references. This wastes space and also the time of the user.
4. In most manuals, unlike encyclopedias, alphabetical arrangement seldom provides room to discuss topics in much depth. Often such books are actually glossaries and are confined to definitions and superficial explanations.

## Ways to Organize

**In Order of Importance**
Vehicle description
Motor
Steering & suspension
Interior
Baggage area

**By Technology**
Summary
Aerodynamics
Propulsion
Structures
Electronics
Reliability
Manufacturing

**By Location**
Overview
Bucket
Crane
Controls
Platform

**By Alternatives**
Summary of problem
and solutions
Alternative 1 (pre-
ferred)
Alternative 2 (less
preferred)
Alternative 3 (least
preferred)

**By Pros and Cons**
Problem and solution
Arguments for
Arguments against
Alternatives

# DOCUMENT DESIGN IN REPORTS

The technical writing profession talks a lot about "docu-ment design," but that does not mean artistic layouts as much as it means structuring the information to make it easy for the user to grasp.

The key to organizing a technical report is hierarchical structure, section by section, right down to the parallel-ism in each sentence. Every element of a document should be linked to the next, like computer code.

In formulating the organization, go "top-down." Progress from the general to the specific. After all these years of touting top-down analysis, even the software in-dustry still produces some manuals that are "topsy-turvy."

But don't employ two or three hierarchies at once; that's worse than no organization at all.

You may want to use some mind mapping. Get a stack of paper, and on each sheet write one main point you want to make. Then under these points you have the room to make sub-points. You can help the author outline a speech or an article or a technical paper with only five minutes of concentrated thinking.

Hierarchy is far more important than sequence. It gen-erally makes little difference whether "wheat" comes be-fore "corn" or after "rice." But "shredded wheat" should be classified under "wheat," not anywhere else. And all topics should go under a summary like "grain."

Companies waste a lot of time trying to decide on the ideal sequence, particularly in new-business proposals. They put outlines up on the wall and pace back and forth, in groups, sometimes far into the night. As they march up and down, they repeat again and again the clarion call, "This should go up front," until the ultimate sequence is decided by the loudest person (or the highest ranking one) and the original structure becomes entirely lost.

This midnight sequencing by committee is an ego trip and a sign of amateurishness. When it gets right down to it, sequencing is not that important anyway. All of the boxcars will arrive at the station at the same time, where they will be split away and shunted off to their proper disciplinary destinations.

# THE IMPORTANCE OF SUMMARIES

As a technical editor, don't let the wasteful walkthroughs bother you. After the smoke clears, just write a good summary, up front, to cover all topics and protect the document's hierarchy.

A good summary can create miracles. If the author has a long, disorganized megillah about, say, horseshoes, bookshelves, and coffee cups, an editor can draw the whole thing together with a neat summary: "The three main items of concern are horseshoes, bookshelves, and coffee cups." And then make sure that the document discusses each one, in that order.

Note how much better this quick solution is than trying to awkwardly explain the diversity, or saying nothing at all. It reflects the overwhelming importance of a summary. But it also teaches a lesson: If writing looks organized, it truly is organized.

## SUMMARIES: FIRST OR LAST?

Note that in technical documents summaries should go at the front. This may bother some literal minded people, because it seems to violate the very principle of "summarization." Perhaps they would prefer a different label for the opening section, like "Introduction" or "Overview" or "Prolegomenon."

You can call it what you want. You may want to use the name of the project. But just make sure that readers don't have to sneak a look at the back of the report to find out who won the game and the final score.

The editor must make the summary blend in with the rest of the report. Too many summaries end clumsily, or lead into still another opening discussion, perhaps called the "Foreword" or "Scope." Such extra sections lead only to bulk and confusion, not elucidation.

After the summary, make sure the author starts giving details right away. Capitalize on the momentum. Continue immediately with an orderly discussion of the selling points the summary has just outlined.

Don't start all over with a "Scope."

## REPETITION: GOOD OR VERY BAD?

Repetition is sometimes necessary, but most of the time it burdens the poor reader with recitations of what he already knows.

There is no excitement in repetition, only dullness and bureaucracy. That old country preacher who proclaimed that he "tells 'em what I'm going to tell 'em, then tells 'em, and then tells 'em what I told 'em" has caused more dull, belabored, turgid writing than even the U.S. government. Many textbooks are written on this pattern, which is one reason they are often so big and expensive with so little content.

This literary technique reveals a monumental contempt for the audience. To write well, you need to envision an audience you like and respect, not one that tolerates tedium.

All right, sometimes you will want to emphasize one particularly important point, as in a WARNING. Or you may reprise an earlier section. But be sure to make it clear to the reader that it is a repeat, and that you are doing it for a purpose. And be sure that your repetition is graceful.

Also, don't end the document with a summation of what the reader has just finished reading. Instead, get the authors to say what the results mean. Ask them to talk about future action—about steps that need to be taken later. Such recommendations may have great interest.

And, by the way, if the recommendations are particularly interesting, they should also be included (in brief) up front in the Summary.

## TECHNICAL WRITING NEEDS SOME RIGIDITY

Technical writing needs rather rigid internal organization. Note the following example.

```
The probe is covered by a multilayer insulation (MLI) blan-
ket prior to entry. Following passage through the entry
heating pulse and deceleration to low supersonic velocity,
the aft heatshield is separated with a small drogue chute.
The main chute is deployed subsonically and the forward
heatshield is jettisoned. The descent module, with the
scientific instruments, continues on the main chute to .the
10-bar pressure level with an option for detachment at this
level.
```

The author needs to make clear what is happening and when, like this.

```
The probe is covered by a multilayer insulation (MLI) blan-
ket. After entry and deceleration to slow supersonic veloc-
ity, the aft heatshield is separated with a small drogue
chute. When the probe reaches subsonic velocity, the main
chute is deployed with the scientific instruments and the
forward heatshield is jettisoned. At the 10-bar pressure
level there is an option for chute detachment.
```

Note that the editor could have shortened the paragraph one more word by cutting out the word *blanket*, but *blanket* creates a good picture of what MLI looks like for the reader.

## THE PROCESS OF DOING A COMPLETE REWRITE

A technical editor often has to do a complete rewrite, using cut-and-paste techniques (either automated or manual).

The first step is to rewrite the outline. This can be done as follows:

1. Find the main points.
2. Form these points into groups.
3. Group the groups, forming a structured hierarchy.
4. Cut up the original copy and paste as much of it as possible into this structure.

Then rewrite the copy, as follows:

1. Chop excess words.
2. Write subheads for the start of each section, and follow with a sentence that sums up the content.

3. Supply summaries for each list and topic sentences at the head of each paragraph.
4. Link paragraphs by using repeated, overlapping phrases, and sentences by using repeated words. (See Chapter 7, "Paragraphs.")
5. Reverse the chopping process and insert appropriate continuity words at the beginning of most sentences (*therefore, however, so, also,* etc.).

Try a storyboard outline if you like. Storyboards are particularly popular on proposals (see Appendix B) and are coming to be suggested for manuals. Just don't spend too much time on them; get on with the writing.

Remember, outlines and storyboards don't have to be firm. You'll have frequent chances to change them as you get more ideas.

## "BAD NEWS" REPORTS

One kind of report that needs to be edited, or rewritten, very carefully is the "bad news" report. In this case it may be appropriate to reverse our earlier techniques and indeed follow an inductive, "building block" approach.

Try to prevent the author from blurting out the bad news. Here, let him tell about his investigation, step by careful step. Let him postulate his requirements, his theories, and his hopes. Then, when he finally reaches the news about the catastrophic plane crash, the inadvertent reversal in the bond market, or the anguishing death of the rabbit, the reader will know that the author tried his very best.

**The "Bad News" Report**
Problem
Unpalatable solution 1
Unpalatable solution 2
Barely palatable solution 3
Upbeat denouement

This reverse style of writing is valuable in communicating both up and down the line in industry, such as when you need to tell your boss that you have to hire some people quickly or the job won't be completed on time, or tell the Air Force that your prototype is 127 pounds overweight, or tell employees that they can no longer use the shortcut through the accounting department.

In bad news reports, there is one more organizational detail. Yes, you don't put the bad news first, but you don't put it at the very end, either.

In the denouement, tell the eager readers about the promise and the potential of Plan B. Tell about the talented young technicians available for temporary transfer, or the resources you intend to explore with the ever-alert QA people to fix that insignificant fuel leak.

End on an up beat, and give readers the sense that you are fully in control and ready to accept this new challenge.

## ABSTRACTS

A few types of technical writing, like articles in some journals, begin with an "Abstract." Abstracts are seldom used in manuals or proposals, and are mostly relics of technical papers or technical reports written by academics or would-be academics.

The abstract, when it is used, has a special function. It is meant to be a separate library reference, telling technical readers what the report is about, in some detail. Most abstracts are from 50 to 250 words, but in some garrulous instances they can run to 1000 words or more.

An abstract is structured differently from a summary. Whereas a summary emphasizes main ideas, an abstract is designed to talk about the paper itself. It is therefore written "linearly," describing each section, as opposed to a summary, which should be written "top down" and describe only the items of most interest.

For example, an abstract is careful to note that the paper includes sections on "Testing" or "Quality Assurance." These, as part of the routine, might escape notice in a summary.

## PREFACES

A preface is a short section at the very front of a document (ahead of the summary) in which the author can talk about his own writing. This is where he gives credit to those who helped him and apologizes for what the document does not attempt to cover. This may be the only humble section in the report.

The preface is really the only section that can be off the subject. All other sections should be focused not on the author's work, but on the subject itself.

## EXECUTIVE SUMMARIES

Executive summaries are popular in large, multivolume reports. They are generally separate volumes that are designed for the top decision makers in the customer organization, and they get special treatment in the way of format, paper, and artwork. For example, for some reason they are likely to be formatted horizontally rather than vertically.

Some of these documents are very elegant, and they tend to be written much better than the basic technical document. They may be the product of professional writers and artists, and may be easier to understand. They offer both an opportunity and a challenge for young technical editors seeking to advance their careers.

Sometimes top priority executive summaries are written by a cabal of 30 or 40 subject experts in an overnight session or a long weekend. The group often invites an editor to sit in, perhaps along with an "administrator" to look after the artwork and keyboarding. In this group of top executives, an editor really has a chance to shine.

In other circumstances, companies may assign the executive summary to a senior editor months ahead of time, perhaps teaming her with a manager who helps with technical decisions. In fact, sometimes a writer/editor can create a job for herself by volunteering to do the actual writing and shepherd the drafts through the long approval cycle.

On the other hand, in the chaos of amateur report preparation, the first author seldom stands a chance; too many people have the irresistible urge to change copy. Therefore, an editor may find it politic to let someone else sacrifice himself on the first draft and save herself to deftly display her manifestly superior talents of revision.

In industry, it's better to be an editor, not a writer. Writers are always criticized harshly, whereas editors are on the side of the critics.

# CHAPTER 5

## Words

What makes one word better than another? Good editing is often thought of as "the right choice of words." In a famous quote, Mark Twain said, "The difference between the right word and the almost right word is the difference between lightning and the lightning bug."

Editors therefore spend a lot of time fiddling around with words. But what actually makes one word better than another?

### SHORT WORDS

There are two types of writing in which words are particularly polished. The first one is advertising. The aim of advertising is to get a message across. To do it, copywriters use short words that paint pictures.

The other one is poetry. Think of a poem you like. Probably, it is full of words that evoke images, like "village," "woods," and "snow." Try writing the same thing with "implementation" and "characteristics" and see what kind of poetry you get. Sir William Gilbert did it successfully, but only assisted by the music of Sir Arthur Sullivan. The result: risibility.

Technical editors are on the horns of a dilemma about vocabulary. Instinctively, they believe, like Johnson O'Connor, a tub-thumper of the 1920s, that vocabulary is an indicator of intelligence and a key to success. They are also attracted to the beauty of words and may have on their shelves at home titles like *You English Words* (John Moore), *The Romance of Words* (Ernest Weekley), and *A Browser's Dictionary* (John Ciardi).

But at the same time, editors realize that the purpose of language is really communication, and that therefore, as editors, they have to tone down writers' ostentatious latinate locutions and write in two-bit Anglo-Saxon words that people can understand.

Does this mean that a varied vocabulary is not useful to an author (or an editor)? Not at all. One of the pleasures of writing is to find the right word, the exact word, the "lightning" that will energize the reader.

"You English words, I know you: You are light as dreams, tough as oak, precious as gold, as poppies and corn, or an old cloak . . . "
—Edward Thomas, English poet and early friend of Robert Frost

In technical writing there is often an evil tendency to consider the reader a moron and to write down to him. That's wrong. Editors need to consider the reader a human being whom they like and respect, and to write directly to that person.

Long words sometimes imply the writer's concern with his own erudition. However, if the long word is the exact word, or one that adds interest and variety to the presentation, we should not hesitate to use it.

If an author has intentionally used a sesquipedalian word, an editor should look at it carefully before changing it to something more bland. See Jacques Barzun (1986) for an author's view of editorial meddling.

## THE TWO KINDS OF JARGON

Perhaps unfortunately, technical writing inherently requires a lot of big words: *autoclave, carcinogen, recidivism*. Some of this jargon we simply cannot avoid. We need it to get our points across. To quote Dr. Earl English, long-time dean of the School of Journalism at the University of Missouri, "To know the vocabulary is to know the technology."

But this necessity also means that editors are needed to slow the writers down in the words they use to connect these jawbreakers.

There are two kinds of jargon. The good kind is the kind that we use to explain our concepts, like *autoclave*. Also, no reader will object to simple words like *tag, marker,* or *nested*; they are easily understood and fit naturally into descriptions of processes.

But the jargon that gives trouble includes words like *schema, abstract base class, database engine*—words that create the wrong pictures or no picture at all. Even more troublesome are the convoluted nontechnical "narrators" found in so many academic papers and textbooks: "It has frequently been noticed by observers such as myself that. . . ."

According to Philip Howard in *The State of the Language* (1985): "Jargon is a Janus-word, looking in two directions, with double meaning. The experimental and physical (sciences) will tend to have more of the jargon that is descriptive, technical vocabulary; the social sciences that deal with the imponderables and unpredictabilities of human nature will tend to have more of the jargon that is gobbledygook."

## ABSTRACTION

One reason that big words are harder to understand is that they tend to be more abstract. Texts are easier to read if you call a spade a *shovel*, not an *implement*, and a building a *factory*, not a *facility*. The more common words create better pictures.

It's always easier to interest a reader in specific facts than in generalities. You can say,

    A period of unfavorable weather set in.

But this is not as good as,

    It rained every day for a week.

Try this:

```
New facilities for research in the field of chemistry will
be in the process of construction during the coming year.
```

Why not say:

```
Next year we will build a new chemistry lab.
```

Notice that the simpler, less complicated language is more specific, less abstract.

S. I. and Alan Hayakawa in *Language in Thought and Action* (1990) show how to build a ladder of abstraction.

You can start with the word *car*. You can make it more specific, more visible, by calling it a *Ford*. Then you can go one more step and call it a *Taurus*, creating a still sharper image. Imagine a ladder with the most abstract word at the top and the most concrete at the bottom:

Transportation

Automobiles

Fords

Tauruses

Note how you can change the image by saying *jalopy* or *Thunderbird*. With each specific new word, you get a different picture.

But unfortunately, in technical writing we too often go in the opposite direction toward the more abstract. Instead of calling it a car, we may call it a *vehicle*. Or we may even call it a *system*.

And then, instead of a *motor*, we run it on a *propulsion system*.

The Hayakawas make one other point, though. They note that good writers do not stick on the bottom rungs of their ladders. Instead, they say,

> The interesting writer, the informative speaker, the accurate thinker, and the sane individual operate on all levels of the abstraction ladder, moving quickly and gracefully and in orderly fashion from higher to lower, from lower to higher—with minds as lithe and deft and beautiful as monkeys in a tree. (111)

## THE CONTROL WORDS

Therefore, as we have seen, vocabulary is often overrated as a tool of good writing. Actually, instead of using large words, writers would be better served by learning to use small ones, especially the "control words." Control words are particularly useful in editing. They are the words that help our structure, and therefore our emphasis and our ultimate overall meaning.

Most of the time, control words are linking words, like *however* or *therefore*. But they can also be adjectives (*only, new*) or adverbs (*now, hardly*). Occasionally, they are large (*indubitably*), but mostly they are small (*too*).

> **Some Representative Control Words**
> accordingly, also, although, always, because, both, but, definitely, even, especially, ever, hardly, however, in summary, more, moreover, mostly, much, nevertheless, new, now, only, on the other hand, overall, so, such, therefore, true, ultimate, unfortunately

The purpose of control words is to show relationships between "content" words. Thus, even though they are smaller and more common, they have the power to assume complete command.

Unfortunately, in technical writing, we tend to minimize the importance of control words, failing to use them or failing to use them correctly. Too often, editors, seeking to cut copy, edit them heavily. But these are obviously the wrong words to cut.

On the other hand, control words are no substitute for good organization. The best and smoothest continuity is offered by logical sequence. In other words, the true strength is in the bricks, not in the mortar.

Nevertheless, an occasional control word can expand the scope of thought, providing, for example, a comparison between concepts, thereby enhancing contrast and sharpening the image.

In fact, control words are so helpful in swaying the reader that when they are used properly they mark the difference between writing that is good and writing that is merely mediocre.

## SEQUENCE OF WORDS

Technical authors, like non-native authors, sometimes do not pay much attention to the natural order of words. But natural order makes a great difference in smoothness, and therefore in understandability.

Here are a few rules of sequence that editors should know. Like most rules, they should not be followed rigidly.

1. Always place determiners first (*the, a, some, my*).

2. Use time before date before place.

   ```
   The meeting is scheduled for 2 p.m. January 6 at the Regis
   Hotel.
   ```

3. Use numbers before judgments before descriptives.

   ```
   A few questionable travel expenses
   The two ugly white flower pots
   ```

4. Use size before shape before color.

   ```
   A little, round, silver medallion
   ```

   (There are many exceptions, chiefly when words have been used together so often that they have become attached.)

   ```
   The spunky little old white-haired lady
   ```

5. Use commas to separate parallel adjectives.

```
Our red, white, and blue flag
A round, red, steel object
```

(Nouns can indeed be used as adjectives.)

6. Break up "stacked" sequences like:

```
Great Neck, N. Y.-based MLG Industries.
```
MLG Industries, based in Great Neck, N. Y.
```
Queen Elizabeth II of England's younger sister
```
the younger sister of Queen Elizabeth II of England

7. Apply "as well as" to the usual, not the unusual.

```
She coaches basketball as well as teaching English.
```

(Unless she is primarily a basketball coach. Then it's vice versa)

## *THE* AND *AND*

Two of the smallest words in the language are also the most often used: *the* and *and*. Good writing uses lots of *the*'s but few *and*'s.

*And* is associated with "doublets" *(prepare and submit, separately and supplementally)*, which can often turn into cliches *(each and every, various and sundry)*. It is also associated with loose sentences, as well as with long ones. You will find a lot of *and*'s in poor engineering writing.

You may even find a few *and/or*s. *And/or* is not conversational English; it is never said except in humor. An airbase newspaper once advertised a dance in which cadets were invited to bring their "wives and/or girlfriends."

But in technical writing, where much misplaced effort goes into ensuring that the language is sufficiently "formal," *and/or* is greatly overused.

It's argued that a writer often needs the "either or both" concept. But *and/or* is not natural English, and is difficult for readers to process. Most times you can simply substitute *and* or *or*, as in the awkward "For each task we choose the best hardware and/or software." Or, if that gambit really doesn't work, simply use "either or both." That's English idiom.

Conversely, poor technical editing will often try to eliminate *the*, going to the telegraphic style to save space. But *the* is a valuable word. It is in the idiom of the language, which is a powerful reason for retaining it. But, more important, it is a "weak demonstrative," helping us to distinguish among nouns, verbs, and adjectives.

English is what is known as an "analytic" language. Unlike Latin, we have few inflections, but depend for our meaning on context. Many words can be more than one part of speech: *switch, can, watch, flush, book.* "Time flies," goes the old joke, with the punch line, "I can't—they move too fast."

Have you ever wondered why headlines are hard to read? Readers need *the* to tell the difference between "the switch lever" and "switch the lever" or "light the exhibit" and "the light exhibit."

After World War II, a prominent journalism school condemned starting sentences with *the*, on the grounds that it was "monotonous." This temporarily led to a rash of stories that began "City council voted Tuesday to. . . ." But *the* does not get tiresome. In fact, it is not even noticed—until you mistakenly leave it out.

## LET THE AUTHORS HAVE THEIR WORDS

The Janus-faced nature of jargon is helpful to technical editors. They can often fix nontechnical jargon, particularly the deadwood.

But when it comes to technical concepts, editors should encourage authors to use their own departmental idiom. A logistics engineer writes differently from an aerodynamicist, and neither of them sounds anything like an engineering psychologist. When the logistics engineer is writing to another person of the same species, he should be allowed—even encouraged—to use the jargon and the trite cliches of their common profession, and not a foreign, sanitized "style-manual" language.

In fact, the editor is well advised to learn that technical lingo and use it herself; it will help her relationships with the technical people.

This gives us an important tip on how to edit based on linguistics. [See Read (1989) and many others.] Don't argue about individual words. Let the subject experts choose their own. Make the editing changes in the structure. Rearrange the sentences, the paragraphs, and the sections, cutting out the deadwood, but do not alter the individual words. Most of the charges of "You changed my meaning" come not from changes in structure but from changes in single words. This is discussed further in Chapter 13, "Getting Along with Authors."

Cutting out the offending words entirely is often more acceptable than changing them! If the copy reads "approximately 40,000 meters," changing it to "about 40,000 meters" may arouse ire. Using just "40,000 meters" is better, because any quantity stated in round numbers is approximate anyway.

This approach can be extended to cutting out whole phrases, sentences, and even paragraphs that do not add to the content, but rather add confusion, taking up valuable time for the reader and soaking up cost. As discussed in Chapter 3, one of the most valuable functions of an editor is cutting copy.

## WORDS ARE TRICKY

We sometimes think that words have one meaning and one meaning only. Most technical glossaries give only one meaning for a word. But almost every word, including proper names and some very specific scientific words, has at least two meanings. Consider *table; class; back; floor; book; light; cup; glasses; watch; flush; right; left.*

An editor needs to be aware of this language phenomenon. Let's see why.

Take the three synonyms, *required, necessary*, and *needed*. Then insert them into a simple sentence:

```
Mechanics are _____ to repair aircraft.
```

Note how each synonym changes the meaning!

"Mechanics are *required* to repair aircraft" means that they have to do it as part of their job.

"Mechanics are *necessary* to repair aircraft" means that no one else can do it.

"Mechanics are *needed* to repair aircraft" means that we need more mechanics.

There are at least two lessons here.

First, an editor has to be very careful in inserting synonyms. It's easy to change an author's meaning.

And second, it is the sentence, not the word, that is the idea module. (See Chapter 6, "Sentences with Style.") The ideas are in the sentence, not in the individual word. That's why the editor needs to study about sentences.

## DEFINITIONS

One of the panaceas routinely offered for attaining precision in choosing words is to supply definitions: If we define our terms, the reader will surely understand.

Definitions are indeed handy. An editor should know that a definition is composed of (1) a genus and (2) a deferentia that distinguishes the item from others in the genus.

To fill the gaps in the *OED, Webster, American Heritage, Random House, Webster's New World,* and others, dictionary makers have created dictionaries of specialties and sub-specialties within highly technical fields ("Last Word in Words," 1993). *Books in Print* lists more than 800 such titles, but even the specialists don't use them much.

In the first place, definitions are stuffy. "According to Webster's dictionary . . ." is among the most trite starts in English prose. (See Chapter 4, on organization.) But definitions are also an unreliable criterion for word meanings.

Dictionary definitions are only points on a broad spectrum. As argued in the General Explanation of the *Oxford English Dictionary*, "vocabulary is not a fixed quantity circumscribed by definite limits." Words can be defined only in context. In technical writing in particular, words have shades of meaning that must be interpolated between the broad stabs made by various dictionary makers. This is part of the technology of English.

We must realize, too, that definitions often define words only in terms of other words. They don't get closer to the object themselves: "A manual" they say, "is a type of handbook."

In technical writing, the best definitions are what Anatol Rapoport (1954) called "operational" definitions, which tell not what things *are*, but what things *do*. Still, editors should not rely only on definitions to paint pictures for their readers.

## WORD HIERARCHIES

As mentioned words can be tricky. As an example, zealous engineers often try too hard to assign exactness according to some pattern. They may have a lot of anxiety about a word like *system*, which technically may include not only an aircraft, but also the pilot, all of the ground support equipment for fueling and servicing, the external fuel tanks and other stores, the communications network, etc. That means the aircraft itself becomes a *subsystem* and the crew station a *sub-subsystem*.

Often an elaborate hierarchy is built up to identify things as systems, subsystems, components, piece parts, details, or items. The trouble is that these terms are not used at all consistently. A lot of people spend a lot of time and money worrying about how to classify various parts of a total system according to some ethereal hierarchy.

Editors know that all of these terms are not names, but classifications. These classifications are constantly shifting according to the needs of the writer and reader. Classifications are "empty" words, devoid of any meaning except in context. A radar set can be, in some cases, a radar *system*, a radar *subsystem*, or a radar *component*.

It doesn't make too much difference as long as the real name is attached. We could call it a radar *thing* and our meaning would come across just as well. (Except that we wouldn't call it that, because *thing* is not part of the accepted jargon.)

Too many times we fret about defining exact classifications for empty words, like *system, configuration, requirements, structure, schema, hardware*. But, to quote Judge Learned Hand, "Words are chameleons, which reflect the color of their environment."

## WORD VARIETY

The technical editor must be aware of one conflict in trying to make technical writing "literature."

A good writer can be distinguished from a clumsy one by the variety she uses in her vocabulary: In her descriptions she may call a spacecraft a *capsule*, a *vehicle*, a *craft*, a *spaceship*, a *ship*, a *conveyance*, an *assembly*, or even a *chariot*.

But beware! If there is ever chance for confusion in design elements—the parts in a manual, the assemblies in a proposal, the nomenclature in an assembly drawing— then the element must go by the same name in every reference, so that the reader can find what he is looking for! To suddenly call the skin a *cover* or the door an *aperture* can cause chaos.

However, only the most pedestrian technical editor will insist that the writer use the same word every time. We must use variety in our vocabulary or risk sounding like "The House That Jack Built."

Variety is particularly applicable when we are discussing a *fixed geometry modular MRS manned re-entry vehicle*. We want to steer away from sentences like this: "The controls of the spacecraft shall be designed to insure that the spacecraft occupants can return the spacecraft to a safe landing with all of the components on the spacecraft surface intact and all of the interior components of the spacecraft as near as possible in working order."

## PRONOUNS

Unfortunately, pedestrian editors may also make war on pronouns. Pronouns are part of good English. Naturally, care must be taken that they refer to the proper antecedents, but that infrequent hazard need not forbid them from being used in the course of writing normal technical English.

By the way, it's time to discard that old nonrule about pronouns referring to the last previous noun. Here's a poorly phrased sentence:

```
Pour lithium into molten glass, and it comes out lighter
and stronger.
```

The author does not realize that *it*, being in the subjective case, seems to attach to *lithium*, the theme of the discourse.

One does not need to go far for other examples. Find the phrase directly above: ". . . care must be taken that they refer to the proper antecedents, but that infrequent hazard need not forbid them from being used. . . ." *Them* clearly refers not to *antecedents*, but to the theme, which is *they*, or *pronouns*.

This pronoun principle also works in the objective case.

```
Protect all decking so weather does not hurt it.
```

You can see that *it* refers not to the last noun, *weather*, but to the last object, *decking*.

## SEMANTICS

Many of the principles concerning words that we have discussed so far are found in the literature of semantics. They are based partly on work by C. K. Ogden and I. A. Richards (1930) and were popularized extremely successfully by S. I. Hayakawa (1941), whom Richards visited shortly afterwards at the University of Wisconsin.

Semantics is essentially the study of labels and how things are named. It could also be called "How words can be tricky," because the "word" is not the same as the "thing." [A useful examination of the relations among "things" (referents), writers, and readers appears in Killingsworth and Gilbertson's *Signs, Genres, and Communities in Technical Communication* (1992).] Each of us has a different concept of the words we use, especially words like "democracy" and "dissent." The object of the editor is to get the writing to conform, as much as possible, to the real world.

In technical writing, many of our arguments can be traced to different interpretations of words such as *manage* or *original* or *analyze*. Definitions don't always work, because they often merely define words in terms of other words. Therefore, one of the useful principles of semantics is to define objects or concepts in terms of what they do. (Rapoport 1954).

If an editor realizes that a disagreement is about labels, he can often simply change the label. A section about "top management" that doesn't address top management can be either be rewritten or the title changed to "key personnel." This will often make everyone happy and bring the report into the real world.

Other handy semantic concepts for editors include classification and abstraction, extremely useful in organizing documents. Also, in proposals, editors must fight the sales department version of glittering generalities, and try to bring bragging paeans down to hard facts. Even in technical descriptions, research, and many other fields, editors must identify the ever-present bias and decide if it is harmful or merely allowable pep talk. In personnel relations, of course, racial, sexual, or ethnic bias can be very harmful indeed.

An editor will learn that many times, truth is in the eye of the beholder. A growing son is a "big" boy, even if he is only 4 feet tall. A "large" attendance may be five people. The "real truth" about Richard Nixon or Ted Kennedy will always vary widely, even in a small group.

Fortunately, in technical writing, we do a good job of pinning "intensional" words like *big* down to "extensional" ones like *5 ft by 5 ft*. That's part of what an editor can do, making the authors stick as close as possible to objective, empirical, solid fact, and use standard measurements so there can be no disagreement in order to create concepts in the mind of the reader that are as hard and unambiguous as tempered steel.

This is why content editing has a much broader scope than grammar and spelling because it must include not only technical detail, but also logic and, to some extent, the complete interface between language and thought.

## ETYMOLOGY

Many technical and academic words have interesting etymologies, or origins. *Algebra* is one of the few words in English that came from the Arabic (*al-jabr*, which meant "bonesetting"). *Ancillary*, from the Latin *ancillaris*, meant "a maidservant." *Anode*, from the Greek, meant "the way up" and *cathode* "the way down"; they are both related to *method*, "the way after."

The word *cleave*, descending to us from Old English, merges two almost opposite meanings, "to adhere" (from *clifian*) and "to split" (from *cleofan*). *Stencil* may have come from a variant of *scintilla*, or "spark," because the original stencils were used by holding them up against the light.

*Conduit*, *ductile*, and *educate*, three widely separate words, can all be traced back to the Latin *ducere*, "to lead." *Matrix* comes from the Latin *mater*, or "womb." Paradoxically, *microphone* means literally "small sound," while *megaphone* means "large sound."

*Gamut*, derived from *gamma*, a Greek letter, and *ut*, the musical syllable "do," became the name of Guido d'Arezzo's "great scale" of all the notes used in medieval music. *Tantalum* came from "tantalize," for its metalworking difficulties. *Nickel* came from the German *kupfernickel*, or "devil copper," false copper.

*Oxygen* was named by Lavoisier from the Greek *oxys*, "pungent," but the acid smell was later found to come from hydrogen! *Ozone* came from the Greek *ozein*, "to emit a smell."

A *campus* was originally a "field," where scholars walked and taught; a *curriculum* was originally a "race course"; and a *symposium* was a "drinking together." The more things change, the more they remain the same.

Here's a brief list of other word origins. You, as a student of words, may want to extend it.

| | | |
|---|---|---|
| *Engineer* | Old French | To contrive |
| *Etymology* | Greek | Word study |
| *Gantry* | Greek | Pack ass |
| *Mathematics* | Greek | Learning |
| *Memento* | Latin | Mind, remember |
| *Molybdenum* | Greek | Silver mingled in lead |
| *Parallel* | Greek | Beside one another |
| *Salary* | Latin | Soldiers' pay to buy salt |
| *Science* | Latin | To know |
| *Spectrum* | Latin | Image |
| *System* | Greek | A whole compounded of parts |
| *Turbine* | Latin | To spin, make turbid |
| *Vellum* | Middle French | Calfskin |
| *Vertical* | Latin | Vertex, peak |
| *Vortex* | Latin | To whirl |

Etymology is not an exact science; it contains a lot of speculation. But it is great fun. A great many, maybe most, of our technical words come from Latin or Greek. Tamara M. Green's *The Greek and Latin Roots of English*, 2nd ed. (1994), shows many such roots in several technical fields.

One prime use of etymology for editors is in spelling, where it may help them to remember that *stationary* comes from "station" but *stationery* from "stationer," the station's storekeeper. In French the *capitol* (building) is masculine and *capital* (city) is feminine. *Personnel* comes from the French "personne." *Iridescent* comes from "iris," and *supersede*, unlike *proceed* or *precede*, is from "sit" or "saddle." *Complement* comes from "to complete" and *compliment* from "to comply." *Accommodate* descends from "commodious" or "commode."

## WHY ENGLISH SPELLING IS STRANGE

The varied sources of English words are responsible for the vagaries of English spelling. Words, as Walter J. Ong (1982) has demonstrated, have acquired more definite visual shapes since the printing press made possible widespread literacy.

Only in the late eighteenth century, as a newly literate public began demanding to know the "right" ways to write, did the publication of books on grammar, usage, and spelling begin. Since 1755, when Dr. Samuel Johnson published the first comprehensive English dictionary, we have relied on dictionaries to give us definitions and etymologies.

## Confusable Words

accede, exceed
accept, except
affect, effect
advice, advise
aid, aide
aisle, isle
alter, alter
bale, bail
bare, bear
bloc, block
born, borne
breath, breathe
calendar, calender
callous, callus
cannon, canon
canvas, canvass
capital, capitol
carat, caret, carrot, karat
cite, site, sight
desert, dessert
discreet, discrete
do, due
dual, duel
eminent, immanent,
    imminent
faze, phase
flair, flare
florescence, fluores-
    cence
formerly, formally
foregone, forgone
hangar, hanger
hoard, horde
its, it's
old factory, olfactory
ordinance, ordnance
personal, personnel
prophecy, prophesy
racked, wracked
right, rite, write, wright
shear, sheer
stationary, stationery
team, teem
their, there, they're

Many people have wanted to simplify English spelling. Noah Webster, setting out in 1806 to make a specifically American dictionary, attempted to substitute *tho* for *though*, trying to make spelling conform to the current sounds of the language. Almost the only spelling reforms of Webster's that stuck are *color* for *colour* and *theater* for *theatre*.

On the British side of the pond, George Bernard Shaw promoted spelling reform in the early twentieth century. He pointed out, in a famous example, that it was theoretically possible to spell *fish* g-h-o-t-i: *gh* as in *enough*, *o* as in *women*, *ti* as in *ambition*.

Now, spelling seems to be becoming much more fluid again. Homophone confusions abound. (A homophone is a word that sounds like the one you mean, but has a different spelling.) Even words that almost sound alike— (e.g., *gibe* and *jive*)—seem to be used interchangeably. In April 1994, a debate raged for days on TECHWR-L, the Internet technical writers' conference, over whether it was "You've got another *think* coming" or "another *thing* coming." Despite the *think* party's citing of the *OED*, the *thing* party continued to insist on its own version.

## WHAT YOUR SPELLCHECKER WON'T TELL YOU

If you as an editor wish to be conservative in matters of spelling (not a bad idea), you should not depend too heavily on a computer spellchecker.

Your spellchecker can't tell you that you've used a homophone. As long as you use spellings contained in its dictionary, it will never beep at you.

The antidote to "howlers" in company documents is not computer spellcheckers, though they're good at finding typos like *depenednt*. The antidote is word knowledge on the part of editors.

Common confusables are shown in the text box.

Editors find such confusions a source of amusement. There was a recent reference to "Pachelbel's Cannon": how would that cannon sound in Tchaikovsky's *1812 Overture*? The phrase "old factory responses" appeared in a news article on the connections between the senses of taste and smell. A community college home economics course has a "duel listing" with social science; more action than the students bargained for, perhaps. A student wrote of puberty rights—the latest entitlement?

Employers are not amused by such confusions.

# CHAPTER

## Sentences with Style

**P**eople like to say that editors work with words. But editors work more with sentences.

Sentences, by definition, are groups of words that express complete ideas. Thus, they are actually the smallest units of thought. They are the "idea modules." In editing, therefore, they deserve the most attention.

In technical writing, each sentence must be clear and precise; it must convey information. Other forms of writing may amuse or inspire, but the prime purpose of technical writing is to inform, to instruct, to explain.

At its best, technical writing possesses a clean style.

Until recently the canon of style, along with those of arrangement, memory, and delivery, received scant attention in technical writing. Technical writing shared the engineering focus on the canon of invention: development of the substance of the argument.

Yet, even back at the start of the twentieth century, the mining engineer T. A. Rickard (1910) exhorted engineers to pay attention to style. Better style, he argued, would promote more efficient reading, and "efficiency is the fetish before which [the engineer] bows continually."

Thus, the object of technical editing is to make sentences more efficient—clear, emphatic, and coherent.

## EDITING SENTENCES FOR CLARITY

For better or worse, sentences are elastic; they can be stretched to include two or three or more thoughts and suggestions, imposed by the author or his technical appenders and qualifiers. They also can curl and twist and convolve and contort and undulate and meander and inosculate. We see a lot of this convolution in technical writing. It's up to the editor to fix it, to beat up on those snakes.

How long should a sentence be? The question remains unresolved. Dr. Harry E. Francis, for many years an editing supervisor at C. F. Braun Corp., Alhambra, California, stated it well: "Anything over fifty words may be unwieldy; anything under one may be vague."

Dr. Francis used to say wisely that "The person who can write a simple declarative sentence can write his own ticket." Why would he need to say that?

Unfortunately, engineers and other subject experts show a marked fear of sounding like "Dick and Jane." Too often they have been taught that the simple sentence is "immature," and they do whatever they can to expand it.

Here's a classic protest of short sentences, written by a 52-year-old electronics engineer in an industrial technical writing class:

```
Some people object to long sentences which in reality indi-
cates they are able to compose sequential thought in writ-
ing consequently these people demand short sentences as a
method of forcing a complete thought into a few words
nevertheless it is possible to use unending sentence struc-
ture which will cause no real concern to the reader pro-
vided that the subject and modifier are not widely separated
and the thoughts are related by by connecting words or
phrases such as consequently, nevertheless, although, which,
or similar type cue words which link sequential thoughts
effectively with a resulting comprehension which is much
greater than sentences 'which are broken by modifying
phrases,' or 'by subjects with obscured modifiers,' or
'similar poor writing practices' 'such as this last thought,'
force the reader to retain the modifiers in memory until he
finds the true subject and thereby limit reader comprehen-
sion by use of long prepositional phrases which disrupt the
thought train as opposed to use of connecting cue words
which tend to link thoughts and provide a thoughtful tran-
sition by alerting readers to qualifying conditions (con-
sequently) or by exception (nevertheless) or by a true
situation (in reality).
    Don't you agree?
```

We don't, of course. Note that even this engineer obviously felt the need for some sentence punctuation, so he used italics.

A good rule of thumb is this: Ask not the number of words in a sentence, but the number of thoughts. If you have a good thought, do not bury it in a tandem grave. Revive it and make it stand on its own in a brand new sentence.

Thus, the first law of editing sentences for clarity is to

## Create one thought per sentence, and one thought only.

What counts as a thought? In its simplest form, a thought is identical to a simple sentence. It contains the *theme* on the lefthand side, and on the righthand side follows the *rheme*, or the action.

```
Arnold (theme) writes technical manuals (rheme).
```

You can, of course, use this simple sentence as a matrix clause (see Chapter 8, "Grammar") upon which to embed other possible clauses:

```
Arnold, a leader of the poetry society during his under-
graduate days at Oberlin, now writes technical manuals for
a small hydraulic-pump manufacturer in Canton. There, he is
able to use the text-layout skills he developed as editor
of a college poetry magazine, although now he chunks larger
units of text.
```

Such embedding prevents an author from sounding like Dick and Jane.

However, many studies have shown that in the past 100 years we have begun to write shorter sentences; any survey of technical reports will prove it. But the reason is simple: instead of commas, we are using a lot more periods. The eighteenth century sentence, divided by colons (which now have a different function), subdivided by semicolons, and resubdivided by commas before rumbling on to a full stop 80 or 90 words later, is out of fashion. Even today, however, some of these grand sentences are still fun to read, and are not too hard to understand. Here's an example:

```
These unhappy people were proposing schemes for persuading
monarchs to choose favourites upon the score of their wis-
dom, capacity, and virtue; of teaching ministers to consult
the public good; of rewarding merit, great abilities and
eminent services; of instructing princes to know their true
interest by placing it on the same foundation with that of
their people; of choosing for employment persons qualified
to exercise them; with many other wild impossible chimeras,
that never before entered into the heart of man to con-
ceive, and confirmed in me the old observation, that there
is nothing so extravagant and irrational which some phi-
losophers have not maintained for truth.
    —Jonathan Swift, Gulliver's Travel's, Part III, Ch. 6
```

The prototypical eighteenth-century sentence had a virtue that often outweighed its apparent vices: it was meticulously well organized. It went straight to its target in a calculated crescendo, often climaxing with a magnificent blast of invective. When well written, it gave no doubt about its clarity.

On the other hand, readers of technical documents aren't there to have their ears tickled by oratorical flourishes. They want information, now! The visual bulk of a sentence like Swift's retards access. Easier access is a good argument for having one thought per sentence.

Another warning for editors is to

## Watch out for strings of nouns!

Here's an example of a noun string.

```
On January 17, in the southern sector of the White Sands
Missile Range, DESTACOM conducted a desert environment night
tank movement infrared sensor detector test.
```

Such strings are common in technical writing. They're often another form of jargon, a shorthanding of longer concepts. But clarity demands that the editor unpack the noun string.

In the example above, the string extends from "desert" to the end of the sentence. Unpacking begins at the rear:

```
. . . test of sensors of infrared illumination, used to
detect the movement of tanks in the desert at night. (Envi-
ronment and detector redundant.)
```

Here's another example of a noun string:

```
An infrared frequency light emitting diode quality testing
facility is currently under construction.
```

Is that "a facility that tests the quality of diodes that emit infrared light?" Maybe not, since "light-emitting diode" (LED) is standard jargon. How about "a quality-testing facility for infrared LEDs"? Be guided in your unpacking by the jargon sensitivity of readers.

Deciding what to cut, as we show in Chapter 3, is one of the editor's key skills. When an engineer cries, "You changed my meaning!" it may mean that the editor has substituted other words for technical jargon.

Here's another guideline for promoting clarity:

## Edit for rigid parallelism.

In a famous paragraph from *Effective Revenue Writing* (1961), Calvin Linton says:

Parallelism . . . is like a comb drawn through tangled locks. Paragraphs which look hopeless . . . can be transformed into neat separate strands by the ordering comb of parallelism . . . parallelism is basic, for it builds rhythm, and rhythm is basic; it demands order, and order is another word for reason . . .

Parallelism eliminates serial redundancy, the sort that occurs when successive sentences add only small bits of information:

```
Disk Doctor checks the disk's FAT sector. Then it examines
the file structure. It also looks for strings of lost
clusters.
```

Three sentences with the same subject but different verbs can be made into one sentence with parallel predicates:

```
Disk Doctor checks the disk's FAT sector, examines the file
structure, and looks for strings of lost clusters.
```

Similar branching can be done with any grammatical structure: subjects ("Stanford and MIT were among the finalists . . ."), verbs ("The F-16s sought out and destroyed their targets"), and prepositional phrases (". . . government of the people, by the people, and for the people").

## EDITING FOR EMPHASIS

Important as it is to cut out useless verbiage, it's not enough to create efficient sentences. Good sentences must have emphasis.

Another law of editing, formulated by George Campbell, Scottish minister and author of *The Philosophy of Rhetoric* (1776), is this:

## "For strength of sentences, never end them with an adverb, a preposition, or any inconsiderable word."

We know that law; it has descended to us in a narrower form in our grammar books. It's good advice for editors, not because of what it prohibits about prepositions, but rather for what it says about the strength of the periodic sentence.

You may have learned in grammar that English has two types of sentences: the loose sentence and the periodic sentence. The loose sentence starts with its main point and tails off. It is a sentence in which the main idea is completed before the sentence is finished:

```
We will have to change our plans if the new procedure is
adopted.
```

The periodic sentence, by contrast, starts off slowly and builds to a climax:

```
If the new procedure is adopted, we will have to change our
plans.
```

We need both types of sentence, but the periodic sentence is ordinarily stronger and more emphatic.

E. B. White picked up this theme in the famous *Elements of Style* (1979). His quotation—or rather the quotation of his mentor, William Strunk, Jr.—becomes a corollary of Campbell's dictum:

## "Place the emphatic words of a sentence at the end."

If we say, for example:

```
At this stage of planning, the wetland has been put at risk
by development of the sports complex.
```

We can make it much stronger by exclaiming:

```
At this stage of planning, the development of the sports
complex has put the wetland at risk.
```

Once again, please note that these are not rules. They are simply laws of natural language. Just for example, an ardent environmentalist might prefer the original casting, strengthened maybe by a home-grown epithet:

```
At this stage of planning, the wetland has been put at risk
by development of this excrescent sports complex.
```

That's what's known as putting the punch line at the end.

Strunk also made another point, familiar to most editors:

## "Use the active voice."

In the sentence "The wood was split by Fred," *wood* is the grammatical subject. *Fred*, however, is the agent. The easiest sentence to read is the one in which the agent is also the subject: "Fred split the wood." But you can use the passive when you want to use your word order to create emphasis, as in ". . . this excrescent sports complex." Note that this distinctly active sentence is framed in the passive voice! There are many uses for the passive voice, as the text box shows.

---

**WHEN TO USE THE PASSIVE VOICE**

The active voice is generally better than the passive ("The boy hit the ball."), but not always. The passive is often shorter, more direct, and more emphatic.

Use the passive voice:

1. To emphasize the agent by putting it at the end.
   "The longest ball *was hit* by a little girl!"
2. To emphasize the action by putting it at the end.
   "I've *been robbed!*"
3. To maintain the theme in a paragraph.
   "Trees are fragile. They can *be hit* by lightning."
4. When the agent is irrelevant.
   "The welfare office has *been moved.*"
5. When the agent is unknown.
   "Something must *be done* immediately!"
6. When an agent does not exist.
   "Soldiers *are* not *made* of steel."
7. To hide the agent.
   "Your new coat *has gotten* dirty."

Note: Many sentences containing *to be* are neither active nor passive:

- Predicate nominatives ("He is a veteran")
- Predicate adjectives ("I am exhausted")
- Also, progressive forms of transitive verbs ("I have been taking medicine") are active, not passive.

---

To create emphasis, you can't usually bolster your technical writing with epithets. Remember that the most effective word in a sentence is at the end. You can say:

    John was slow, painstaking, and meticulous.

Fine. That's a nice compliment for John. But suppose you say:

    John was painstaking, meticulous, and slow.

That could get John fired.

There's another principle to observe:

## In any sentence, put lists at the end.

The sentence above is a right-branching sentence; John's three qualities come at the end, or on the right side of the sentence.

If we rephrased it: "slow, painstaking, and meticulous was John," we would have a left-branching sentence. A poetic example is "Black, black, black is the color of my true love's hair."

Believe it or not, you can also have sentences that are middle-branching, but they are complex, contorted, and convoluted as in this sentence itself, hardly an example of clear writing.

The preferred branching for technical writing is generally the righthand one. Right-branching sentences have the advantage of orienting the reader immediately. If the unfortunate reader encounters: "The aileron, the flap, the wing, the fuselage, and the empennage are all parts of an aircraft," she has to wait until the end of the sentence for any idea of what the author is talking about. But if the sentence starts, "An airplane includes . . . " the list of parts causes no confusion.

The right-branching sentence has another advantage: it can continue for as long as one wants, although monotony could be a problem.

There is also a corollary to this rule:

## Put the longer item at the end of the list.

An example: "He installed the door, the windows, and the rest of the flooring." You can see how confusing it might be to reverse the order: ". . . the rest of the flooring, the windows, and the door." Note that this rule can be violated if you want specifically to show the sequence of installation.

You will also make more sense if you:

## Avoid duffel bag sentences.

Lists are an important part of technical writing, but, like anything else, they must be organized. Too many miltary people write duffel bag sentences, with hardware items stuffed in among materials, structures, actions, and responsibilities. If, instead, you group similar items together, your lists will be more orderly.

Note, for example, "Information covered includes human characteristics, abilities, limitations, physiological needs, performance, body dimensions, biomechanical dynamics, strength, and tolerances." Apples and oranges. But start with *body dimensions*, group together *biomechanical dynamics* and *tolerances*, then *strength* and *performance*, then *abilities* and *limitations*, then *human characteristics* and *physiological needs*, and, presto, you're more readable.

Duffel bag writing can also lead to technical errors like "Coverage extends to the survivability, vulnerabilty, and lethality of targets."

## EDITING FOR COHESION

Sentences don't work in isolation. They need to connect smoothly one idea to the next if readers are to develop the understanding the writer intended. That is, sentences need to cohere.

We have already seen that active sentences lead to sentence clarity. However, in *Style*, Williams sets the priorities between sentence-level clarity and overall cohesion thus:

> The problem—and the challenge—of English prose is that every sentence requires us to find the best possible compromise between the principles of clarity and directness . . . and those principles of cohesion that fuse separate sentences into a whole discourse. **But in making that compromise, we must always give priority to cohesion; to what fuses sentences into cohesive discourse.** (boldface Williams's)

Williams insists that cohesion comes from moving from the familiar to the unfamiliar, from the old to the new.

This convention is often violated in technical prose. According to George Gopen and Judith Swan (1990), in "The Science of Scientific Writing,"

> in our experience, the misplacement of old and new information turns out to be the No. 1 problem in American professional writing today. The source of the problem is not hard to discover: Most writers produce prose linearly (from left to right) through time. As they begin to formulate a sentence, often their primary anxiety is to capture the important new thought before it escapes. Quite naturally they rush to record that new information on paper, after which they can produce at their leisure the contextualizing material that links back to the previous discourse. Writers who do this consistently are attending more to their own need for unburdening themselves of their information than to the reader's need for receiving the material. (555)

Structural clues to meaning include both side-by-side juxtaposition and overall order. Juxtaposition tells us which of several possible meanings a word most likely has in the given context: hot soup, hot pepper, hot item. Order enables us to extend our understanding by moving us successively from the familiar to the unfamiliar.

Since writers don't pay enough attention to how readers construct meaning, that chore is left to editors. Here are some hints on editing for cohesion:

### Give your reader the context.

As you work with engineers and other technical people, you'll probably notice that they speak to you as if you were fully familiar with whatever they're talking about. They're usually thinking about the problem at hand, not about your need to understand it.

When they write, they do the same thing. Sometimes it would help if they'd just drop a hint to help you get oriented.

Imagine a sentence like this:

```
Fenway has a really short left field fence.
```

That sentence is clear if you know a little about Boston and baseball, but some readers might need a little more context:

```
Fenway Park, Boston's American League baseball stadium,
has a short left field fence.
```

In reports in industry, the early part of the first sentence should contextualize—should let the reader know how this writing connects with the reader's interests. The readers are not always the ones the writer expected, so detail is usually appreciated.

If the reader is overseeing several projects in the conductive materials department as well as chairing the division's personnel review committee and serving on the long-range planning committee, contextualizing lets her snap into character and to figure out what this memo requires of her.

In the following abstract of a scholarly presentation, contextualizing would help make clear what sort of space is to be compressed:

```
In this paper, a dynamic space compression method called
DSC is proposed. The basic idea of DSC is to construct the
compression circuits by dynamically estimating error prob-
abilities of the outputs. Experimental results demonstrate
that DSC is very efficient. The theory to predict the
performance of general space compression methods is devel-
oped and is verified by simulation results.
```

A few context words would also alert the reader that the intended audience is computer scientists:

```
Magnetic data-storage media can be used more efficiently
through dynamic space compression (DSC). DSC constructs
the compression circuits . . .
```

One important part of contextualizing is this:

## Put the "framework" of the sentence at the beginning.

The framework includes circumstances of time, place, or condition: "In the beginning . . . ," "In Chicago . . . ," "Despite the rain. . . ."

In addition, of course, you should:

## Put any linking words at the very beginning.

These are words like *nevertheless, moreover,* or two of the most popular words in technical writing: *therefore* and *however.*

Note that sentences can indeed be organized in an infinite number of ways, but one smooth, natural order is:

Linking word, framework, subject—predicate, and the items in the list, with the longest item at the end.

Now let's see what we have in a representative sentence:

```
Therefore, in Chicago the most important things to see are
the Sears Tower, the Field Museum, Wrigley Field, and the
Gold Coast along Lake Michigan.
```

## EMULATE THE INCHWORM

Achieving cohesion also means paying a lot of attention to how sentences begin and end. That means you must emulate the inchworm.

The inchworm moves along by anchoring one end and extending the other into new territory, then anchoring and extending again. Similarly, sentences should start with the subject, old territory, then extend themselves into new territory on the right or predicate side. In the sentence after that, what was the new territory becomes the old territory—the subject—and the predicate again extends itself into new territory.

The inchworm strategy assures that the reader advances along smoothly, not having to leap forward and jump back to make connections:

```
Today, the president signed into law Congress's compro-
mise budget. Though this budget raises taxes on the
president's favorite constituents, he had come to view
the congressional compromise as the best available al-
ternative. The only other alternative, a veto, would have
invoked the Gramm-Rudman automatic spending cuts. The
resultant indiscriminate chopping of federal programs
would most likely send an already shaky economy into deep
recession.
```

A confusing paragraph that appeared in an electrical engineering textbook, did not follow the inchworm strategy. Its writer evidently had the "Sommerfield model" at the forefront of his mind, so that's what came first:

```
The Sommerfield model gives a satisfactory representation
of most of the electronic properties of metals. We have
just seen a few examples of this in the preceding section.
This justifies a posteriori the assumption of this model
that the electrons move freely; i.e., they are subjected to
a constant potential in matter. However, it is well known,
by x-ray diffraction experiments in particular, that met-
als have a crystal structure. The electrons should there-
fore be subjected to a periodic potential with a period
that should be related to the size of the unit cell. We
must therefore conclude that this periodic variation in
potential is small in metals and can be neglected.
```

What should have come first is a reference to the preceding section that allows the reader to regroup before being introduced to the apparent anomaly of the crystal structure in metals. Also, this writer has loosened coherence by using *this* to refer to no particular concept named in the preceding sentence.

*This* should alert editors to another coherence issue:

## Keep an eye out for anticoherence viruses.

In computerdom, a virus is a string of code that a computer processes like a normal one but which messes up the programs it gets into. In prose, an anticoherence virus is a normal-looking part of speech that a reader processes normally but which messes up the reader's ability to make sense of a passage.

One strain of anticoherence viruses can be screened by simply paying attention to a handbook rule:

## "Make a pronoun refer to a specific antecedent rather than to an implied one." (*Little, Brown Handbook,* 5th ed., 1992, 12c)

This rule is worth following, because it generally improves coherence. The usual suspects are the demonstrative pronouns *this* and *that*, their plurals *these* and *those*, the relative pronoun *which*, and the simple pronoun *it*.

```
A mathematical analysis and computer simulation will be
used in the investigation of air drilling. This will pro-
vide a practical approach . . .
```

What will provide—analysis, simulation, or investigation?

An unadorned *this* at the beginning of a sentence often signals a coherence problem. To fix it, supply the antecedent:

```
This simulation will provide a practical approach . . .
```

Let's see how we can revise the "Sommerfield model" paragraph.

1. Contextualize by putting the reference to the previous section first.
2. To solve the problem of the nonreferent *this*, use *these examples*.
3. In the original, *however* alerts us to a contradiction. Move *potential* to the head of the sentence to sharpen the contrast.
4. Make "in each a structure" inchworm off of the previous sentence's "crystal structure."
5. Use "variation" to inchwork off of "varies."

Here is the revision:

```
In the previous chapter, we saw a few examples showing that
the Sommerfield model satisfactorily represents most of
the electronic properties of metal. These examples justify
a posteriori the model's assumption that the electrons move
freely, subject to a constant potential in matter. This
```

```
potential might be expected to be periodic, since x-ray
diffraction shows that metals have a crystal structure. In
such a structure the period of the potential varies in
relation to the size of the unit cell. However, in metals
this periodic variation is so slight that it can be ne-
glected.
```

These repetitions help us to **get the story straight**, as discussed later in Chapter 7, "Paragraphs."

Stories work only when they focus on some particular theme or concept. If that theme is named as the subject of most of the sentences, the prose passage will gain in coherence. If the story is about a scientist, her name goes first as the subject of most of the sentences. If the story is about the work, work becomes the subject. Note that the latter case may require you to use passive voice.

You will remember that back in Chapter 2, "Editing for Content," we said that an editor can sometimes use her knowledge of English structure to sort out the gobbledygook.

In the original draft of the Sommerfield copy, the author committed a strange but common fault of technical people: he used *therefore* instead of *however*.

Examine the last two sentences in the original: "The electrons should therefore be subjected to a periodic potential with a period that should be related to the size of the unit cell. We must therefore conclude that this periodic variation in potential is small in metals and can be neglected."

An editor will know that the *therefore* in the last sentence does not make sense; only when she substitutes *however* does everything line up logically.

Thus, simply by knowing sentence structure, an editor can correct technical copy in an important way, without knowing anything at all about "periodic variations in electrical potential." And the technical people will thank her for it.

---

**CONTROLLING RAMBLING SENTENCES**

To control rambling sentences, cut long sentences into shorter ones and recombine them to adjust emphasis, putting key words where the reader can find them. Use the following techniques to attain clarity, cohesion, emphasis, and conciseness:

- Generally avoid the passive voice.
- Use the theme-rheme concept, with:
  - The theme near the beginning.
  - The emphatic point at the end.
- In every action, make the agent clear.
- Prevent smothered verbs.
- Unscramble noun strings.
- Eliminate redundancy.
- Delete pompous diction, obvious statements.
- Minimize asides to the reader.
- Eliminate excessive negatives.

## FOG INDEXES

If you follow the advice in this chapter, you can be reasonably sure that your prose will be readable. You can check your readability, of course, by using a grammar-checking software package. These packages can be useful if you're aware of their limitations.

Software grammar-checkers use algorithms like that of the much maligned "Fog Count." The Fog Count assays to measure readability by counting the number of words per sentence and the percentage of words of more than two syllables. It then uses a formula to determine the school grade level at which you are writing. The actual formula, including embellishments and qualifications, can be found in Robert Gunning's *The Technique of Clear Writing* (1952) and in a widely distributed Gunning pamphlet, *How to Take the Fog Out of Writing* (1964).

The father of readability indexes was Rudolf Flesch, who was not a writer but a psychologist and who in 1943 published his Ph.D. dissertation as *The Marks of Readable Style*. No one should criticize readability studies without having first read Flesch's rationale, which is based on extensive historical data, on tests of long sentences, and on the influence of affixes on abstractness (departing from a host of earlier studies, such as those by Thorndike, on word frequency or familiarity).

Critics of readability studies maintain that writers shouldn't try to write to a formula. And they are probably right. Even mathematically inclined engineers do not ordinarily like the Fog Count, complaining that it ruins their "natural style."

But editors, working "after the fact," can occasionally use the formulas as an impartial way of pointing out wordiness and obfuscation, thus helping to break down the barriers to heavy editing.

Another criticism is that readability studies make no attempt to measure "understandability." But Flesch answers that complaint in the first paragraph of his first best-selling book, *The Art of Plain Talk* (1946). Plain talk, he explains, is "how to speak and write so that people understand what you mean."

After World War II, Flesch became a national sensation, revitalizing the *Wall Street Journal,* the Associated Press, and many magazines. He left a lasting mark on journalism, by insisting on an opening paragraph of no more than 19 words.

"How can we do that," complained old-time newspapermen,"and still get in the five W's and H?"

Flesch's answer was simple: "Put some of them in the second paragraph."

His influence has endured. You now see the five W's and H used only in an occasional news lead; they survive mainly in sales meetings and in business school lectures on how to write a news story.

Flesch lived to a prolific old age, producing at least 17 books, and he has to be counted as one of the greatest influences in the twentieth century on business writing.

In fact, he may have influenced technical writing a bit too much, instilling in young writers a positive terror of big words, thereby perhaps dampening their vocabulary.

But today, for good or bad, readability indexes are used heavily in computerized style checkers and also in military manuals, where the "grade levels" are taken seriously. Nowadays, word and sentence lengths are measured by keystrokes, allowing instant calculation.

Here's a tip for military editors: the indexes are much less sensitive to long words than to long sentences.

Readability is an asset in technical writing, particularly in new-business proposals, where your competition may unwisely scorn it. Some companies unaccountably talk down to the customer with vapid slogans, repetitions, and over-explanations, while at the same time objecting to "insulting his intelligence" with short words and short sentences.

## READABILITY PRINCIPLES

In this book, we have not consciously used any readability indexes. Nevertheless, we think it will be understandable to a wide range of users, from college-educated and post-graduate readers to people for whom English is not their native language.

Here are some of our own readability principles:

- We have tried to speak directly to our audience, envisioning you as people we like and respect.
- We have tried always to be logical, believing that logic is the foundation of all good writing, and especially technical writing.
- We have tried to organize well, grouping topics into logical chapters and sections and using informal preludes to introduce the problem or approach.
- We have tried to use the paragraph as an organizational device for grouping thoughts and segregating the groups. We have tried to keep our paragraphs short. Often, instead of paragraphs, we have used lists.
- We have tried to organize sentences well, believing that organization is more important than an arbitrary word count. We have indeed tried to restrict our muse, though, to one thought per sentence.
  - We have tried to begin each sentence with the theme under discussion and end with the main point.
  - We have put the real subject and the real verb in their honored places, rather than in phrases.
  - We have tried not to over-qualify.
  - We have used right-branching sentences.
  - We have observed strict parallelism.
- We have not hesitated at all to use long words, even technical ones, but have tried to explain them as we went along. (Note, however, that we use few formal definitions.) In contrast to too many technical writers, we remain committed to the value of vocabulary.

- – We have tried to write in the idiom of the language, even venturing occasionally into slang. Conversely, we have tried to avoid jargon, unless it was in the common idiom.
- – We have preferred finite verbs (root verbs) to participles and gerunds.
- – We have used extensively the little "control words," or continuity words, knowing that despite their size they have the power to control thought.
- • We have used punctuation liberally.

# CHAPTER

The paragraph is one of our most important vehicles for achieving logic and clarity. But it has to be rated as the most neglected writing device in the technology of English.

# Paragraphs

What are paragraphs, anyway? What are they for? Why do we need them?

Paragraphing is a tool for organization. Paragraphs are particularly useful in "macro editing," which deals with structure, sequence, classification, emphasis, and the whole process of actually getting the point across to the reader.

## THE NEED FOR ORGANIZATION

A report is structured like this:

Sections

Subsections

Paragraphs

Sentences

Each section starts a new subject, and the subsections divide the sections into convenient lengths. The paragraphs then separate the topics within the subsections, placing the sentences into neat groups.

When an author puts a sentence into a paragraph, she is addressing a particular topic. Then, whenever she starts a new paragraph, she is signalling that she is changing to a new topic. This is a vital aid to reader understanding.

That's why paragraphs are far more necessary to the document organization than, say, the decimal numbers and subhead levels that are given so much prominence in style manuals. You'll note that most writing gets along easily without decimals and subheads, but never without the organizing device of paragraphs.

Therefore, no matter how tight the page limit, editors must gently resist the common urge among technical people, salespeople, artists, and keyboarders to cleverly squeeze paragraphs together to "save space."

## THE NATURAL FUNCTION OF PARAGRAPHS: GETTING THE STORY STRAIGHT

The next passage is reproduced from a textbook, with some punctuation added for clarity. It has two stories: the first about sinusoidal waveforms; the second about the aims of the chapter.

```
A common form of voltage and current waveform is the sinu-
soidal type used in main supply systems. Sinusoidal wave-
forms are also encountered as carriers for radiocommunication
systems, and many other waveforms, including continuous
non-sinusoidal signals and audio signals, can be consid-
ered as sums of a number of sinusoidal signals at different
frequencies and amplitudes. In most circuits, it is only
the steady-state response to such waveforms that is of
interest, and this allows the development of techniques not
involving differential equations. We shall first examine
the nature of sinusoidal waveforms and then, by reference
to the fundamental relationships for v and i, investigate
these relationships for the currents and voltages in the
passive elements. Alternative methods for describing these
relationships will be introduced and used for the analysis
of simple circuits. Finally, the calculation of power dis-
sipation resulting from alternating signals will be dis-
cussed.
```

A second story, beginning "We shall," deserves its own paragraph.

Since it's fairly easy to see that the second story is about the chapter, we can gain comprehension by making *chapter*, or a pronoun referring to it, the subject of the rest of the sentences.

Inchworm strategy (Chapter 6) is also needed to move prose along. Since "alternating currents and voltages" connects with the chapter title, we move that to the front of the first sentence. The concept we want to introduce is sinusoidals, so we'll move that to the end. The resulting first sentence:

```
A common form of alternating voltages and currents, used in
main supply systems and radiocommunication systems and
analyzable as a component of other waveforms, such as con-
tinuous nonsinusoidal signals and audio signals, is the
sinusoidal waveform.
```

That's a periodic sentence with a vengeance. It packs too much material into the middle. Readers of English expect to find the verb fairly close to the subject. But this sentence bulges in the middle like a python that has swallowed a pig. So we split it into two sentences.

By inchworming the second sentence, then using a parallel structure to get the rest of the story straight, we can (1) keep the contextualization and (2) move from familiar to unfamiliar. "Sinusoidals" has become the theme of our story, so we want to keep it up front in the rest of the passage.

Here is the result:

```
A common form of alternating voltages and currents, used in
main supply and radiocommunication systems, is the sinu-
soidal waveform. Also susceptible to sinusoidal analysis
are waveforms such as continuous non-sinusoidal signals
and audio signals which can be considered as sums of a
number of sinusoidal signals at different frequencies and
amplitudes. In such waveforms, only the steady-state re-
sponse is usually of interest, so it is possible to develop
analytic techniques that do not use differential equa-
tions.

We shall first examine the nature of sinusoidal waveforms
and then, by reference to the fundamental relationships for
v and i, investigate these relationships for the currents
and voltages in the passive elements. Next, we will intro-
duce alternative methods for describing v-i relationships
and use them to analyze simple circuits. Finally, we will
discuss the calculation of power dissipation resulting from
alternating signals.
```

"Keeping stories straight" involves deciding where they begin and end.

## THE DIFFERENCE BETWEEN WRITING AND EDITING PARAGRAPHS

Editors have a different feeling about paragraphs than writers. Writers commonly follow a building-block approach, constructing each paragraph around a topic sentence and stacking the paragraphs together, either chronologically or "top down." (See Chapter 4, "Document Organization.")

By contrast, editors are not builders; they are fixers. They are not on the assembly line; they sit under the shade tree and tinker (sometimes by the light of the moon, of course). Thus, they don't build paragraphs; they shape them. They receive a long string of copy and employ paragraphing to separate the sentences into cohesive, logical groups. To editors, *paragraph* is a verb.

Instead of perceiving copy as successive stacks of building blocks, editors are more likely to envision the stream of words as an ongoing concrete ribbon, a superhighway. They paragraph not so much to enhance individual edifices as to remove bumps, fill gaps, and insert flexible joints that let that continuous ribbon stretch and contract while remaining firmly intact. Good paragraphing helps the reader travel smoothly, without undue interruption.

In short, editors, in contrast to writers, think of paragraphs not as discrete units, but as parts of a continuing, unified whole.

## TOPIC SENTENCES

In English instruction we hear a lot about topic sentences. Sometimes this idea is even extended into the notoriously rigid "five-sentence paragraph."

Indeed, every paragraph needs a topic sentence. Moreover, in technical writing that sentence should probably go right at the start. But just as important as the paragraph's internal structure are the connectives at each end that allow paragraphs to function as segments of superhighways.

Of course, you can follow whatever editing metaphor you choose. You may personally prefer to liken a paragraph to a cathedral, with myriad intricate, alfresco ornaments that need your special delicate fashioning in order to attract the important reader.

But if you are a true reader's surrogate, you will find you have to devote most of your attention not to individual words but to the big picture, and must strive hard to achieve overall organization, emphasis, and continuity. If, every day, you have to chisel your way through 50 pages or so of somebody's misshapen concrete, sooner or later you're likely to lay aside your delicate and sensitive tools and try dynamite.

Then, to rebuild, you are going to need paragraph connectives. So hang loose and wipe the dust off your glasses; we'll tell you what we mean.

## CONNECTIVES

In constructing coherent sentences, writers often learn to use the inchworm (or theme-rheme) concept, making the end of one sentence become the beginning of the next. The same technique works for joining paragraphs.

Note the connectives between the few paragraphs you have just finished reading under "Topic Sentences":

- "superhighways" - "metaphor"
- "reader" - "reader's surrogate"
- "dynamite" - "rebuild"

The main difference between paragraph continuity and sentence continuity is that for paragraphs you need a heavier splice. Walter S. Campbell (1950) calls the technique "overlapping paragraphs."

The advantage of that heavier splice is easy to prove. The next time you edit a woman's resume, use "she" throughout. But then, when you change the topic with a new paragraph, use "Miss Smith." This simple trick almost always provides more order and unity.

Note, though, that if that next paragraph changes the subject entirely, a simple splice may not be adequate. You may need something less subtle, like a subhead, or at least a *Very Important Introduction:* "Up to this point we have covered half of our subject. The other half . . ." These few words, directed to readers at a different "level of discourse," give them an idea of where they are.

## LEVELS OF DISCOURSE

In the world of computers we are learning how to use multiple levels of discourse, with menus, windows, and hypertext networks. We are learning how to write in new dimensions that break the linear chain and often add access and understanding.

But actually, that approach is not new. For ages, you may have noticed, writers have been been interrupting themselves to talk directly to the reader: "Meanwhile, back at the ranch . . ."

Interruptions are an inherent part of technical writing. One prime example is tables or graphs; these are clearly a different level of discourse. Other examples are equations and quotations and inserts.

In technical writing, though, the way we handle discourse is often clumsy. Technical authors may not be able to keep two things going at once. They may even have trouble arguing two sides of a question, pro and con, back and forth. So it's up to the editor to help them out by providing effective discourse management.

One way to manage discourse is with paragraphing that clearly identifies individual topics, singles some of these topics out for special attention, and very occasionally talks to readers to keep them from getting lost. Making the levels of discourse crystal clear is one of the seldom-mentioned duties of a good macro editor.

## WHAT PARAGRAPHS DO FOR THE WRITER

We have seen how paragraphs help the reader. They help organize his mind; he knows where to file the facts in his head because the paragraphs are feeding them to him in orderly, well-sequenced packages. Readers are lost without good paragraph organization; it tells them what they can safely skip.

What paragraphs do for the writer is add emphasis. They help her make her main points. They are far more powerful than exclamation points or underlines or italics or all caps. Such mechanical devices compete with each other for attention (see almost any user manual), and moreover make the author appear adolescent.

Paragraphs supply their own inherent emphasis. They are part of a hierarchy: a phrase offers more emphasis than a word, a sentence more emphasis than a phrase, and a paragraph more emphasis than a sentence.

Therefore, if you want a reader to remember a very important point, honor it with a separate, v.i.p. paragraph.

## ONE-SENTENCE PARAGRAPHS

Despite what many people think, one-sentence paragraphs are indeed permissible. For example, a good one-sentence paragraph is perfect for introducing a sequence of ideas, as in the Constitution of the United States: "We the people. . . ." At other times, as mentioned, a single, separate, sentence can be used to add emphasis or address the reader at a different level of discourse.

Sometimes a series of one-sentence ideas can be grouped together into one paragraph. But the smooth writer will find that if one of those ideas has *two* sentences, this pair will be more effective if they are allowed to be alone together in one paragraph.

For particularly effective emphasis, imaginative editors also use single sentences or phrases in magazine-type sidebars. Instead of burying an example deep in the body of a long article, they repeat it, bring it out, enlarge it, and give it a border, thereby breaking up the lengthy narrative and adding interest.

## HOW LONG SHOULD PARAGRAPHS BE?

How long should paragraphs be? That question is almost unanswerable. Fashions change. Until the 19th century, according to *The Oxford Companion to the English Language* (1992), paragraphs tended to comprise long periodic sentences, one sentence sometimes taking up a whole paragraph. Some paragraphs would cover one or more pages. But nowadays, writers who want their material to be read, such as advertising copywriters, make their paragraphs short.

Technical writers should learn to use short paragraphs. Edmond Weiss (1991) says, "Business readers are skimmers; many go weeks at a time without reading a paragraph all the way through." Veteran proposal evaluators admit the same thing. Like students in school, they have learned to skim documents by reading only the first sentence in each paragraph. If your paragraph has something to say to a proposal evaluator, the opening sentence is the place to say it.

Weiss goes even farther. "Whenever possible," he says wisely, "multi-step procedures should appear in itemized lists or word tables." This practice is the basis of the new "information mapping" technology.

## THE FLEXIBILITY OF PARAGRAPH STRUCTURE

Paragraphs are essentially an undisciplined bunch. Even as important as they are, they are really governed by only one immutable rule, and that is that no paragraph rules are immutable. This tractability may be one reason why in school we don't learn as much about paragraphs as we do about the picky rules of grammar, which, for good or ill, often seem engraved on tablets of stone.

Nevertheless, despite the wide flexibility of paragraphs in size and function, few writing devices can exceed their rock-hard structural importance in helping editors establish organization, create emphasis, maintain smooth transitions, and develop logical, unified arguments. We need to rescue them from neglect.

# CHAPTER

To make technical documents clear, emphatic, and coherent, you need to understand the basic principles of grammar, and particularly sentence structure. Editing without that understanding is like "fixing" a car by jiggling that thingamajig up by the whatchacallit: might work, might not— who knows why?

Editors have two main uses for grammar: (1) it helps them figure out what's going on in sentences that seem out of control and (2) it gives them terminology to use in justifying their changes to authors.

Not everybody learns grammar in school these days. Many people, under the influence of newspaper columnists who worry about the "degraded" state of the language, identify grammar with those picky rules elaborated in stylebooks. Real grammar, though, helps you take sentences apart and put them back together again, with authority.

## Grammar

✍

"Grammar, like the Sabbath, was made for man, not man for grammar."

## HELPFUL GRAMMAR FOR RESTRUCTURING SENTENCES

It's not much of a mystery why people avoid grammar. When they went to school, if they diagrammed sentences, they probably did their branching and underlining according to rules based on Latin, which works differently from English. Many people can see no practical value in learning such arcane stuff.

But starting in the late 1950s, linguists began looking at grammar in new ways. Noam Chomsky's *Syntactic Structures* (1957) led to the development of transformational grammar, which describes the basic English sentence (S) as consisting of a noun phrase (NP) and a verb phrase (VP), and regards all other sentences as transformations (Figure 8.1). There are only a few of these transformations, and they follow definite rules that children acquire through use, usually before the age of six. Note that we can all speak idiomatically without being able to explain how our sentences work.

**Basic English Sentence**

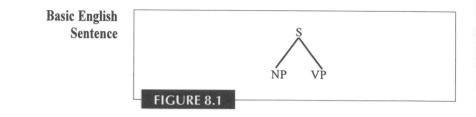

FIGURE 8.1

Transformational grammar can help editors with a wide range of structural problems, from sentence convolutions down to commas and hyphenation.

One advantage of transformational grammar is that it recognizes that English often uses groups of words to perform single functions, whereas Latin and its direct descendants use single words with inflections. For example, in the Spanish word *pensabas*, the *-abas* ending is the marker for both the imperfect tense and the second person. In English, we have to use four words to say the same thing—"You used to think."

Traditional English grammar tries to parse the three words separately, each as a particular part of speech. Obviously, the words do not function separately.

Consider, for example:

```
We cannot put up with any further delays in production.
```

Are *up* and *with* prepositions, or is *up* an adverb because *delays* is the object of *with*? Or does it really matter how they're classified so long as we understand their function? Many people get impatient with grammar because it seems to get caught up in such basically insoluble and pointless questions of classification.

From a transformational viewpoint, *put up with* functions as a single transitive verb, equivalent to *tolerate*.

It's this willingness to look at word strings as single functional elements that gives transformational grammar an analytic advantage for editors.

Or how about a sentence such as this?

```
Thousands of homeowners will take advantage of this offer.
```

Traditional grammar wants to regard *thousands* as the subject, leaving *homeowners* the object of the prepositional phrase. But *homeowners* clearly is the agent in the sentence. Transformational grammar considers *thousands of* to be a type of pre-article called a "determiner," and the whole noun phrase *thousands of homeowners* the sentence's subject. Moreover, as in the previous example, there's a multiple-word transitive verb: *will take advantage of,* the lexical equivalent of *will accept* or *will exploit.*

For editors, the most helpful feature of transformational grammar may be its analytic framework. Those who want a thorough, yet brief, explanation of the grammar should consult *Doing Grammar,* by Max Morenberg (1991).

As Morenberg says,

> Since a small number of structures and operations will produce all the sentences in the language, then your job as an analyst is clearly defined: to learn what those structures and operations are, so that you will be able to analyze any sentence in the language, no matter how long or complex it might become.

Good advice for technical editors.

## Sentence Constituents

A sentence must contain a noun phrase and a verb phrase:

    S = NP + VP

That subjects don't have to be single nouns is a fact most people already intuit. NP may be a single noun, or a noun with modifiers, a transformed verb, or an embedded clause. VP is the verb string (auxiliaries, verbs, and particles), along with objects, complements, and modifiers—what's traditionally called the "predicate."

NP and VP can include other noun phrases, verb phrases, adjective phrases, and adverbial modifiers.

## Basic Sentence Patterns

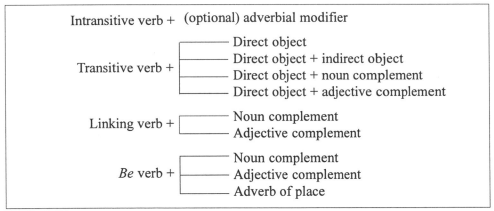

Sentences have a limited number of basic structures, determined by the kinds of verbs they use. Morenberg (1991) lists six patterns; Martha Kolln (1994) lists ten. In both cases the patterns are variation on the four basic verb types listed below.

    Ed eats with gusto. (Intransitive with adverbial modifier)

    Ed eats escargot. (Transitive with direct object)

    Ed passes Mary the wine. (Transitive; direct and indirect objects)

    Ed considers Mary his friend. (Transitive; direct object with noun
                                   complement)

```
Ed thinks Mary cheerful.
```
(Transitive; direct object with adjective complement)

```
Ed became an engineer.
```
(Linking; noun complement)

```
Ed became pensive.
```
(Linking; adjective complement)

```
Ed is a mechanical engineer.
```
(*Be*; noun complement)

```
Ed is helpful.
```
(*Be*; adjective complement)

```
Ed is in his office.
```
(*Be*; adverb of place)

Every English sentence is based on these ten patterns. If one of these patterns isn't lurking within a group of words between periods, it isn't an English sentence.

## Verb Transformations

Verbs are the trickiest parts of sentences. In the first place, every verb has five forms:

| Form | Functions | Examples |
|------|-----------|----------|
| base | verb, infinitive | eat, to eat; work, to work |
| *-s* | 3rd person singular | eats; works |
| *-ed* | past tense | ate; worked |
| *-en* | past participle | eaten; worked |
| *-ing* | present participle, gerund | eating; working |

Three of the verb forms can function as other parts of speech:

```
Ed likes to work.
```
(Infinitive as noun, direct object)

```
Ed needs a working phone.
```
(Present participle as adjective)

```
Working is Ed's delight.
```
(Gerund as noun)

```
Ed has a worked silver ring.
```
(Past participle as adjective)

If a verb form is functioning as a noun or adjective, you can tell by its position and the kind of question it answers. Adjectives often fall between articles and nouns, so they can be pegged by position (a *working* phone, a *worked* silver ring); they also answer "what kind of" questions (Ed needs *what kind of* phone?). If they're acting as nouns, they'll answer "what" questions (Ed likes *what*? *What* is Ed's delight?) If they're parts of the verb, they'll answer "do" questions (Ed *does/is doing/has done* what? Works/is working/has worked).

Verb strings in untransformed sentences always follow this formula:

```
T+[M]+[have + -en]+[be + -ing]+base+[particles]
```

Brackets indicate optional parts. In this system, there are only two tenses, present and past. The tense marker (T) always falls on the first verb in the string. In the four-word verb string in *Ed might have been kidding us,* the tense marker is on *might*, past tense of the modal *may*.

Modals (M) express conditions such as futurity, certainty, and possibility. Modals include will/would, shall/should, do/did, must, may/might, can/could, used to, have to/had to. They usually lack the five parts of normal verbs ("He shoulds" or "she is musting" aren't English). Modals, if present, are always first in the verb string and carry the tense marker. (Ed *might* eat.)

*Have* + *-en* gives us the "perfective" (completed) aspect of a verb string. The *-en* (with regular verbs, actually an *-ed*) attaches to the next verb in the string, transforming a base form to a past participle. (Ed has eaten.) If there is no modal, the tense marker falls on *have*, as in "Ed had eaten" (past perfect).

*Be* + *-ing* gives us the progressive aspect. The *-ing* attaches to the next verb in the string, transforming a base to a present participle. (Ed is/was eating.) If there is no modal or *have* auxiliary, the tense marker falls on *be*.

By combining parts of the formula, we get the "synthetic" tenses:

```
Ed will calculate volumes.
```
 (Present conditional)

```
Ed would calculate volumes.
```
 (Past conditional)

```
Ed has calculated volumes.
```
 (Present perfect)

```
Ed had calculated volumes.
```
 (Past perfect)

```
Ed is calculating volumes.
```
 (Present progressive)

```
Ed was calculating volumes.
```
 (Past progressive)

```
Ed has been calculating volumes.
```
 (Present perfect progressive)

```
Ed had been calculating volumes.
```
 (Past perfect progressive)

```
Ed will have calculated volumes.
```
 (Present conditional perfect)

```
Ed would have calculated volumes.
```
 (Past conditional perfect)

```
Ed will have been calculating volumes.
```
 (Present conditional perfect progressive)

```
Ed would have been calculating volumes.
```
 (Past conditional perfect progressive)

Because this system has only two tenses, present and past, traditional grammar's future tense becomes a present conditional. (Philosophically, the future is inscrutable, so considering the future tense as a conditional actually makes sense.)

The final optional component of verb strings is the verb particle (make *up* a story, put *out* a fire). The particles resemble prepositions, but you know that they are part of the verb string if you can replace the base and particles with a single verb. In the earlier example, we were able to replace "put up with" with "tolerate."

If you're editing copy that is to be read by non-native speakers, it is usually better to replace idiomatic phrases like *put up with, look after, look up to, pull one's leg* with the single-word equivalents *tolerate, supervise, admire, jest*.

## Structural Ambiguity

Verb particles in idiomatic phrases, besides baffling non-native speakers, are responsible for one kind of structural ambiguity. Consider the sentence "Ed works with Mary on the General Widget account" (Figure 8.2): The sentence can be correctly diagrammed in two ways. That is, *works with* could be a verb phrase, or *with* could be a preposition.

Another structural ambiguity results when an indirect object cannot be distinguished from an object complement:

```
Ed found Mary a good housekeeper.
```

In the top diagram in Figure 8.3, Vg, denotes a transitive verb with both a direct object (DO) and an indirect object (IO). Sense: Mary needed a housekeeper.

In the second diagram in Figure 8.3, Vc indicates a transitive verb with a direct object that has a complement (Obj. Comp.). Sense: Ed found Mary to be a good housekeeper.

For editors, being able to explain structural ambiguities is another tool in the arsenal for dealing with authors who can't see a need to change their sentences.

**Structural Ambiguity**

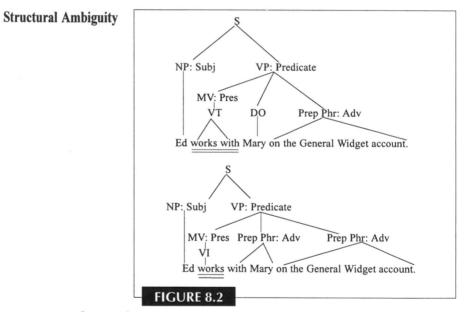

**FIGURE 8.2**

# Sentence Transformations

So far, we've seen that all basic English sentences can be generated by using a few basic patterns. The sentences themselves can undergo a limited number of transformations.

Sentences can become **imperative** by chopping "you" and a modal off the front:

```
[You must] Eat your peas.
```

Sentences can become **negative** by inserting "not" after an auxiliary verb:

```
Ed is not calculating stresses.
Ed calculated stresses ⇒ Ed did not calculate stresses.
```

(When there is no auxiliary, we have to supply one.)

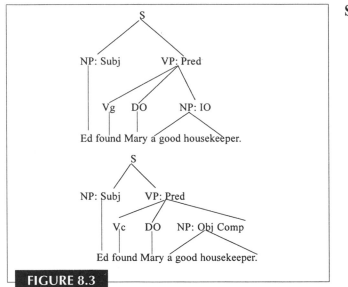

**Structural Ambiguity**

**FIGURE 8.3**

Sentences can become **yes/no questions** by moving an auxiliary verb to the front:

```
Ed calculated stresses.  ⇒  Did Ed calculate stresses?
```

Sentences can become **Wh- questions** by moving to the front a *wh-* word (who, what, where, when, why, how) that stands in for a noun phrase or adverb phrase in the predicate:

```
Ed is moving [somewhere].  ⇒  Where is Ed moving?
```

Sentences can become **passive** (Figure 8.4) if the direct object is made the grammatical subject. (Only transitive verbs can become passive.)

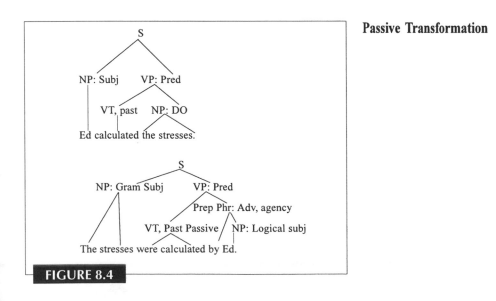

**Passive Transformation**

**FIGURE 8.4**

```
Ed calculated the stresses. ⇒ The stresses were calculated
[by Ed].
```

Passive sentences often contain a verb with the *-en* (past participle) ending. A passive sentence is always recognizable by the *be* + *-en* form at the end of the verb string.

If you include all possible verb elements, a passive verb string can get complicated—

```
The old couch might have been being kept for sentimental
reasons.
```

—but the last item in the passive verb string (except particles) is almost always *be* + *-en,* or in this case, *-t.*

Sentences can be transformed into **existential there** sentences by moving the logical subject behind the verb and replacing it with "there (Figure 8.5)." The reason for using such a structure is that English prefers its predicates to be longer than its subjects. A sentence such as

```
Many spectacular national parks and monuments are in Utah.
```

sounds distinctly odd. It would sound more natural as

```
There are many spectacular national parks and monuments in
Utah.
```

**Existential There Transformation**

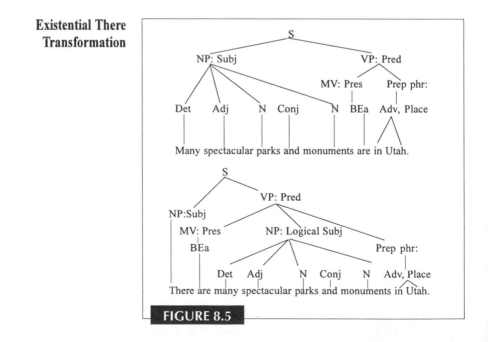

**FIGURE 8.5**

*There* and *it* constructions are useful for putting important words in stressed positions:

```
In Utah there are many spectacular national parks and monu-
ments.
```

Finally, sentences can be transformed by **compounding**. This technique eliminates redundancy:

```
Ed calculated volumes. Ed calculated stresses. ⇒ Ed calcu-
lated volumes and stresses.
```

## CHINESE BOXES: EMBEDDING SENTENCES WITHIN SENTENCES

The transformations discussed so far have produced only simple sentences. Sentences become more complex by embedding other sentences within them. And just a few methods of embedding can account for all the complexity.

The ability to combine sentences by embedding is an important way to control pace and emphasis. Editors have to learn to disembed sentences, because technical prose is highly embedded.

On the other hand, consider the following sentences:

```
Emily went to college.

Emily studied physics.

Physics has several branches.

One branch is quantum mechanics.

Emily liked quantum mechanics.

Quantum mechanics challenged Emily.

Emily liked challenges.
```

Such a string of simple sentences is inefficient. It is much better to turn some of them into phrases or single modifiers, or even to omit the obvious. Some alternatives:

```
Emily, who liked challenges, studied quantum physics.

Quantum physics provided challenges, which Emily liked.

Emily studied quantum physics because she liked challenges.

Liking challenges, Emily studied quantum physics.
```

Sometimes, to edit a sentence, you have to find the matrix (main) clause, to which all the other transformed clauses cling.

The first type of embedded clause is the relative clause:

```
Men are golfers. Men wear funny pants. ⇒ Men who are
golfers wear funny pants.
```

Relative clauses can be further reduced—to participial phrases (present and past), to prepositional phrases, to adverbs, or to adjectives.

```
Passengers hold tickets. Passengers may board. ⇒ Passen-
gers who hold tickets may board. ⇒ Passengers holding
tickets may board. ⇒ Ticket-holding passengers may board.
⇒ Ticketed passengers may board.
```

## CLAUSE REDUCTION AND PROBLEMS IN READABILITY

Some reduced embeddings can cause readers trouble. Often, editors try to treat superficially (with punctuation, hyphenation) matters that are really problems of embedded structures.

In Chapter 6 we showed how to unscramble noun strings. We were actually disembedding phrases that had been reduced to single adjectival modifiers.

Consider a sentence like

```
The company is installing a new relational database manage-
ment system.
```

This can be analyzed as one matrix clause and several embedded ones:

```
The company is installing a system. (matrix)
```

```
The system is new.
```

```
The system manages databases.
```

```
The databases are relational.
```

"Relational database management system" is jargon, a handy shortening of what could be a cumbersome construction.

Recognizing implicitly the unitary nature of such noun strings, technical people often further reduce them to initialisms:

```
Save your scanned image as a TIFF file.
```

Here, TIFF shorthands the noun string "tagged image file format," which can also be disembedded. Technically, there's redundancy in "TIFF file"—but in the contortions you'd have to go through to get rid of it, you would lose much clarity.

## USING TRANSFORMATIONAL TECHNIQUES TO FIX SENTENCES

If you find that the prose you're editing plods along in monotonous sentences, your ability to disembed clauses enables you to put them back together with variety. It also enables you to exploit more easily the coherence techniques of Chapter 6.

Some sentences that you intuitively recognize as bad can be reconstructed after disembedding. Consider this one:

```
Visual observation of the waterflood displacement mecha-
nisms after asphaltene precipitation are shown to be simi-
```

```
lar to the mechanisms of displacement of the unprecipitated
crude oil.
```

Where is the matrix clause in that sentence? It looks like two men in a horse cos-tume, only they're wearing half-costumes from different horses:

```
Visual observations are shown to be similar to mechanisms.
```

That's faulty predication, and to fix it you have to figure out what the matrix clause is supposed to be. Because we recognize a passive structure, *are shown*, we know there's an agent lurking nearby. From the *-ion* ending, we recognize *observation* as a smothered verb. Somebody has observed something; we could make that "somebody" the agent:

```
Petroleum geologists observe [something].
```

If "petroleum geologists" were the subject of the story (Chapter 7), we'd rebuild the sentence on that matrix. More likely, though, our matrix clause should be

```
[Some kind of] mechanisms are similar to [other kinds of]
mechanisms.
```

What to do with the agents? We can embed one of them as a sentence modifier:

```
[Some kind of] mechanisms, visual observations show, are
similar to [other kinds of] mechanisms.
```

Sentence modifiers are mobile; we can place them for best emphasis. Now all that's left is to re-embed the modifying phrases:

```
After asphaltene precipitation, visual observations show,
the waterflood displacement mechanisms resemble those of
the unprecipitated crude oil.
```

In this case we've reduced "mechanisms of displacement" to "those."

## CONJUNCTIONS

Compound and complex sentences are held together by conjunctions, which may be the most confusing part of speech for technical authors. It's up to editors to straighten them out.

There are three types of conjunctions: coordinating conjunctions, subordinating con-junctions, and conjunctive adverbs.

Coordinating conjunctions are easy. There are three principal ones:

*and, but, or*

They are used between clauses in "compound" sentences—"Muriel sang *and* Grace played guitar"—and in series of nouns or phrases. The only punctuation they some-times need is a comma: "red, white, and blue."

Less frequently, *so, only*, and *yet* act as coordinating conjunctions between main clauses. Yet some readers object to their playing that role, so use caution.

The words that make "complex" sentences complex are the subordinating conjunctions:

| | | |
|---|---|---|
| although | as though | where |
| though | as if | when |
| provided that | as well as | whenever |
| given that | so that | however |
| unless | before | while |
| if | after | because |
| as | until | since |
| than | in order that | that |
| lest | | for |

Subordinate clauses cannot use a semicolon, but introductory ones ordinarily require a comma: "Although the weather was warm, the wind was cold." Some teachers say that a comma is not required when the dependent clause follows the independent clause. But most editors use it, especially when the dependent clause is nonrestrictive. ("The weather was warm, although the wind was cold.")

Some subordinating conjunctions can also act as prepositions, and are followed by an -*ing* form in sentences like "He closed the store, as well as opening it." Inexperienced editors sometimes attempt to make the participle parallel to the main verb ("He closed the store as well as opened it.")

Even further confusion comes from some overlap between subordinating conjunctions and conjunctive adverbs: "I will help however I can." Here, *however* acts as a subordinating conjunction. But in "They could not solve the problem; however, they tried," *however* acts as conjunctive adverb.

The conjunctive adverbs include:

| | | |
|---|---|---|
| therefore | then | however |
| thus | also | still |
| hence | besides | otherwise |
| consequently | furthermore | nevertheless |

Conjunctive adverbs can, furthermore, be inserted into the middle of a sentence with surrounding commas; however, if they introduce a clause, they require a preceding semicolon (or period). This may be the most common sentence mistake that technical editors encounter.

## THE CHANGE TOWARD DESCRIPTIVE GRAMMAR

In order to edit technical copy successfully, editors, instead of acting like wrist-slapping "language police," must think more about audience and communication. In technical copy, grammar is simply not a major problem, especially compared to the terrors of wordiness, obfuscation, and general gobbledygook. So, rather than worrying about split infinitives and the ultimate preposition, editors must concentrate on things that are more vital, especially technical accuracy and clarity.

Recent years have seen a sea change from prescriptive, rulebook grammar to descriptive grammar, or the way educated people actually use the language. [See Edward Finegan, *Attitudes Toward English Usage* (1980); Dennis E. Baron, *Grammar and Good Taste: Reforming the American Language* (1982)]. You can trace the grammatical evolution from Theodore Bernstein's first book, *Watch Your Language* (1958), to his *Miss Thistlebottom's Hobgoblins* (1971). In the latter book he implies the relaxation of such older doctrines such as not using *trustworthiness* for reliability (rely-upon-ability?), *retrieve* for redeem, *likely* for liable, *many* for numerous, *type* for ilk, *several* for respective or various, *extraordinary* for phenomenal, *virtually* for practically, *odd* for peculiar, etc.

Similarly, from 1969 to 1992, even approvals by the conservative American Heritage Dictionary usage panels have risen as follows: *intrigue* as a verb from 52 percent to 78 percent, *contact* as an adverb from 34 percent to 65 percent, *aggravate* in the sense of "irritate"from 43 percent to 68 percent, *anxious* in the sense of "eager" from 23 to 52 percent, *transpire* in the sense of "happen" from 38 to 58 percent, and *cohort* as a single individual from 31 to 71 percent.

True, nothing can hurt an editor's career more than a grammatical error. It's just that we have to be sure that in the search for consistency we aren't making things tough for ourselves by adhering to standards that actually violate the rules of idiom and discourse.

## COMPUTERIZED SOLUTIONS?

In technical writing, as writing prowess has yielded more and more to keyboarding skills, grammar has come to be dominated by computerized solutions. But sadly, computers, while being excellent proofreaders, are poor grammarians. In *Macworld*, August 1991, Charles Pillar reported that four grammar programs gave him wrong or borderline answers more than 60 percent of the time. The reason is that grammar is not like algebra. "Unfortunately, or luckily, no language is tyrannically consistent," says Edward Sapir (1921). "All grammars leak." Grammatical rules can therefore be carried to the point where they sound funny.

Most people would agree. Among our most ardent language cops are the Sunday supplement grammar rule-givers. But even the conservative William Safire (1994) has begun to defend "It's him."

## THE AMAZING DIFFERENCES IN ENGLISH TEACHERS

In 1992, Dennis Baron, a linguistics professor at the University of Illinois, published an opinion piece in *The Chronicle of Higher Education* wondering why those people pushing cultural diversity in universities seemed intolerant of linguistic diversity. Of the several replies the *Chronicle* printed, only one seemed to understand Baron's point. That was from an English professor. The other respondents, not professors of English, spoke of the need to uphold "the rules."

As editors well know, everyone is an expert on grammar: artists, word processors, managers, and especially production managers. They all studied grammar in high school and all have individual pet peeves, which makes the subject highly subjective and very controversial.

But grammar is too complex to be covered by high school expertise; you have to know the high school rules, but since you don't want your English to sound funny, you also have to be aware of exceptions made for common usage.

This attitude is nothing recent. Way back in March 1949, *Harper's* published a survey querying 468 people on 19 sentences (including "It's me."). Perhaps the most interesting point was the amazing differences in opinion among English teachers: The 155 college English teachers were the most liberal, whereas the 32 high school English teachers, especially those in small towns, were among the most conservative.

Editors, by the way, were about in the middle.

Today we see a great deal of liberal leadership toward what Janet Rankin Aiken called back in 1936 *Commonsense Grammar*. Fern Rook, a Fellow of the Society for Technical Communication (STC), is a prime example, with her book, *Slaying the English Jargon* (1992). The STC membership tends to be conservative, but one of the most popular panels at STC annual conferences, composed of Lola Zook, Alberta Cox, Eva Dukes, and the late Mary Frances Buehler, has taken a liberal stance. Also, STC has helped temper the bans against split infinitives and prepositions at the end of sentences and has consistently discouraged "obsolete" strictures like *was graduated*.

Now we technical editors must ask ourselves: Are other standards also becoming obsolete? Do we spend too much time moralizing about rules that are no longer valid? Likewise, does our obsession with consistency make our editing too rigid, to the point that instead of "preserving the beauty of the language" we make it sound funny?

Unfortunately, the principal danger to technical copy today may not be grammatical errors as much as grammatical arthritis, an internal buildup of rules that hinders our writing flexibility.

But certainly, to cure the painful buildup we shouldn't abandon the rules, but instead study them.

## FOUR NEW RULES

Much moralizing today centers on four taboos: *data is*, *none are*, *hopefully*, and *which* in restrictive clauses. Ironically, none of these four prohibitions were taught 60 years ago. They are not even mentioned in Aiken or in other books of the period. Thus, instead of an effort to preserve the language, we are witnessing a campaign to impose rigid new rules that would compel us to write "None of the apples is rotten."

That's not good English. It sounds funny.

Here are the sometimes surprising arguments against the four new rules, 1 through 4.

1.  Way back in 1927, *Science* magazine argued that the *data* we know is not the plural of *datum*, which is a word employed only in surveying. *Data*, said *Science*, is a separate collective noun, generally used in the singular.

True, *data* is plural in Latin. But so are *agenda, opera, insignia, graffiti* (It.), and *erotica* (Gr.). In *Webster's Tenth Collegiate Dictionary*, *erotica* has the same notation as data: *n pl but sing or pl in constr.* But we don't say, "Erotica are disrespectful to women." That's not good English.

Some people argue that if one thinks of *data* as comprising more than one element, it's plural. Then what about *sugar* or *coal*, which include many grains and lumps? Are they plural, too? No.

Here's a proven approach. We have two kinds of nouns in English: "count" nouns, like *apple*, which can be pluralized with cardinal numbers, and "mass" nouns, like *sugar*, which depict a singular mass. *Data* is not a count noun, because we can't say "two data"; that's not good English. Thus, you can surmise that *data* is a mass noun, and singular.

One caveat: Some organizations, like science labs, use *data are* (although they may shoot themselves in the foot by using *data point* and *amount of data*, both singular constructions). *Data are* is not better English, but it does make some authors feel better. As a technical editor, don't swim upstream. You can use *data are*. It is never incorrect to follow the idiom of educated people; that's what is called "common usage."

2.    Contrary to popular belief, *none* did not come directly from *not one* but from the Old English *nan*, which was regularly used in the plural. Like *any*, which came from *an* (one), it can indeed be plural, as in Agatha Christie's *And Then There Were None.*

3.    *Hopefully* is a recent prohibition, emerging particularly in *Paradigms Lost,* by John Simon (1980). But it is generally used in an "absolute" or "disjunctive" sense, as one might use *regretfully, clearly,* or *undoubtedly*. In "Clearly, the water is muddy," the word *clearly* modifies only the sentence and has nothing to do with the water. Hopefully, this prohibition will decline.

4.    The ban on the restrictive *which* was made up suddenly by H. W. and F. G. Fowler in *The King's English* (1907). This spurious rule, which dismayed other grammarians, had no background in usage and cannot always be followed, notably in "that which" clauses.

      *Which* has a certain weightiness that is popular with engineers and also with sensitive poets; it has a heavier emphasis, which fits certain meters ("To that pure look which honors paradise," says Joseph Auslander). Its restrictive use is not inherently ungrammatical.

      Anyway, poor Fowler didn't realize how futile it might be to try to stem the tide of engineering *whiches*. Better that an editor save her strength for more important battles.

By the way, the usage panel of the new *American Heritage Dictionary* (3rd ed., 1992) endorses both *none are* and the restrictive *which*. Moreover, it gives *data is* a 77 percent approval.

On the other hand, its approval of *hopefully* nosedived from 44 percent (1969) to only 27 percent. But even *American Heritage* must be leery of this one. Since *hopefully* is used by educated people all around us, the usage panel seems to reveal not as much about correctness as it does about usage panels.

Usage panels are indeed notoriously rigid, often seeing mistakes where there are none. People who are polled know the strangest rules! Zook and her friends (above) often poll their STC audiences. Results are overwhelmingly prescriptive, some people even treating the poll as a quiz on their own knowledge of the rulebook. Respondents should not be asked, "Would you accept this error?" but rather, "Do you notice any errors in this example?"

By bringing supposed rules to people's attention, language critics seem to evoke a response more conservative than people's actual practice. In "The Phenomenology of Error," Joseph M. Williams noted that many prominent upholders of rules elsewhere violate these very same rules. And Williams's article itself contains about a hundred deliberate "errors" that most readers will not have noticed because they are part of the common idiom.

## HOW TO BE A HELPFUL EDITOR

True, all of us are haunted by the ghosts of our sixth grade teachers. We still need standards.

Yes, but whose? Even H. W. Fowler did not always teach good English. The distinguished Otto Jespersen, who wrote the first definitive grammar of English (in seven volumes), called Fowler an "instinctive grammatical moraliser," one of those who "think what excites their particular dislike is something that . . . was not found in the good old days"(1926).

Thus, maybe Fowler himself is one reason, although certainly not the only one, that we have so many stiff, automatic rules; they are made for the moralizers. Indeed, many of the early prescriptive grammarians discussed by Finegan and Baron were also ordained ministers.

Grammar is intensely faddish. But, as preached by one eighteenth-century grammar book, "Grammar, like the Sabbath, was made for man, not man for grammar."

Grammar must be sensible, and based on communication. As editors, eagerly zapping the copy of our peers, we need to ask ourselves, are we really interested in communication, or in improving our zapping average? Are we really being helpful editors?

## THE GROWTH OF ENGLISH

One thing we don't need ever to worry about: English is not decaying. It has grown to be spoken by no fewer than 300 million people, and by over 300 million more as a second language.

But English does indeed change. Just in the past few years we have introduced words like *floppy disk, video, software, gay,* and *sexism.* Conversely, we no longer *motor* in our *auto*, we *drive* our *car*. And we may have lost *omnibus* forever! This is a tangible decline. But where are the guardians of language? They are out Fowlerizing a tiny corps of words like *hopefully*.

Why don't we set up a universal stylebook? That may be impossible. We editors are not about to give up our grammatical independence. Technical writers use expressions that horrify their literary cohorts, and vice versa. Through the years, while we would have liked to find greater mutual agreement, we have always rejected the idea of an academy that sets grammatical standards like the one in France.

## WHERE TO LEARN ABOUT GRAMMAR

How can an editor tell what grammar is "acceptable"?

First, don't rely on any book that has in its title *complete, correct,* or *pitfalls*. Find one that discusses gray areas like countable nouns, *shall* and *will,* the subjunctive, and exceptions to the singular *each* and *either.*

One such book is *Webster's Dictionary of English Usage* (1989), named "Best Reference Source 1989" by the American Library Association. It tells the history of each controversial term, so the background is clear. A smaller one is *Practical English Usage* by Michael Swan (1981). Somewhat different is *The Oxford Companion to the English Language* (1992). Its 1184 pages contain wonderful things.

Grammar is more tricky than most technical people know. We freely use sentences like "We need younger management, who know computers." Is *management* singular or plural? (See "Where Are the Rules When You Need Them?" below.)

Therefore, a second way for us to learn about grammar is to listen. In our content editing, we can keep our brains turned on and follow the natural idiom that does not stem from carelessness but that staunchly follows the educated consensus. This may keep our writing from sounding funny.

We can also consider our readers. If, for a specific audience, authors use *undelete* or *a design criteria,* we may want to improve communication by adopting their lingo.

True, we do need standards. But, to quote William Safire, (1993) "Beware of the shibboleth masquerading as a rule." We must somehow eschew arthritic rigidities that lead us to say "It's I" or "None of the apples is rotten." Our audience will no longer believe what we are saying if they think we sound funny.

## WHERE ARE THE RULES WHEN YOU NEED THEM?

Are these sentences "right" or "wrong"?

```
   1. The police have information on who commit what crimes.
   2. Who will edit this report? I shall. Shall I?
   3. For a whole day, 1200 calories are not many.
   4. She joined IBM in 1987 to help them write their
      manuals.
```

 5. The increase in actuators and the addition of hydralic
    nozzles simply mean we need more control circuits.
 6. Men and women each has their own point of view.
 7. He moved the template 5/16 inch. 0.3125 inches.
 8. We need management who likes to use computers.
 9. Every person does their own work.
10. Ethics is the one major consideration.
11. The EPA has gathered an enormous amount of data.
12. Our management like to use computers.
13. A total of 157 people have registered.
14. He is an electronic engineer.
15. My umbrella has shrunken in the rain!
16. I would like to have found you awake.
17. Was there a rise in your check this week?
18. The entire total of 157 people has registered.
19. Was there a rise in unemployment this week?
20. Plastics is one material that softens with heat.
21. His ethics are unquestionable.
22. Graffiti are a problem for some neighborhoods.
23. Which are never wrong, the rules or idiom?

These are questions that arise frequently among editors. Please note that it is not possible to answer "consistently."

## Answers and Comments

1. *Who* is clearly plural, but the plural *commit* sounds funny.
2. *I shall*, albeit correct by the will-shall rule, sounds stilted. But *shall I?* does not.
3. The quantity 1200 calories takes a singular, like five dollars and 25 years of service.
4. *Their* is frequently used for singular companies or agencies, without objection. This usage is standard British, though Americans often want to call companies *it*.
5. The "increase" and the "addition" seem more like one thing than two. (But note *seem* in this answer.)
6. Despite the rule, *have* is more natural.
7. Despite the rule in technical writing, we ordinarily say "point-three-one-two-five inches," and linguists say "the spoken language is the language." However, we seldom say "five-sixteenths inches."
8. *Management* is thought of as plural here, and as singular in Sentence 12. So both of the sentences sound funny.

9. *Their* is sanctioned by the National Council of Teachers of English, to avoid the awkward *his or her*.
10. *Ethics* can be either singular or plural. See 21.
11. If *data* were really plural, you would say number, not amount.
13. *Have* seems more natural, as does *has* in Sentence 18. Grammatical number is evidently governed by the article!
14. Electronics. Electronic engineers go, "Beep-beep-beep."
15. *Shrink* has two past participles, *shrunk* and *shrunken* (as in "shrunken head.")
16. A clear error. "I would have liked to find . . ."
17. *Rise* is British. Americans use *raise* for pay and *rise* for unemployment (as in Sentence 19.)
20. *Plastics* is both singular and plural.
22. *Graffiti* is generally singular in English.
23. Idiom. (Rewrite the sentence to avoid a trap like this.)

## EDITING TECHNICAL WRITING

1. In a sentence, put the "old" at the front, the "new" at the end.

   `Collecting samples is the first step in pollen studies.`

   In pollen studies, the first step is to collect samples.

2. Make the end of one sentence the topic of the next.

   `Ten of our plants are potential users of Coritone. There are, however, a number of environmental obstacles to overcome before Coritone can be used as a boiler fuel. This year will see the completion of environmental tests.`

   Ten of our plants can potentially use Coritone. However, before Coritone can be used as a boiler fuel, we must overcome a number of environmental obstacles. Environmental tests will be completed this year.

3. Prefer right-branching sentences.

   `One doctrine states that punishment deters as its certainty, severity, and promptness increase.`

   One doctrine states that punishment deters in proportion to its certainty, severity, and promptness.

4. Use one thought per sentence.

5. Put the verb next to the subject.

6. Use active voice—but not absolutely always.

7. Put the main thought in the main clause.

8. Follow parallelism.

9. Avoid smothered verbs.

10. Avoid stacked modifiers.

11. Beware of doublets.

12. Paragraphing:

    Bundle sentences together with connected themes.

    Use paragraph splices.

    Start a new paragraph at a new theme, new scene, new group.

13. Organization:

    Prefer deductive (top down) to chronological.

    Put general before special, simple before complex.

    Group related things together.

14. Keep copy short, but also smooth and idiomatic.

15. Learn from descriptive grammar, not the pop grammarians.

# CHAPTER

**9**

As an editor, you'll certainly have at hand a number of reference books [e.g., *Harbrace* (11th ed., 1990), *Little, Brown* (5th ed., 1992), *Blair* (1994)]. When you're in doubt about punctuation, you should consult one of them.

Their rules, however, are not eternal and immutable. And besides, if you try too hard to apply them mechanically, it can distract you from more important matters.

# Punctuation

## USE ENOUGH PUNCTUATION

Sometimes if you have to get a job out the door by 5 p.m., you can't restyle the sentences. But maybe you can improve clarity just by including some punctuation. Consider this passage.

```
If while these toxic substances are
being transported by rail the tanker
car positive seal filler and inspec-
tion hatch should be inadvertently
left unsecured allowing atmospheric
moisture to commingle with the con-
tained substances reaction of the tox-
ins with the moisture may result in
the escape into the atmosphere of
toxin bearing mists.
```

In such a sentence, where an editor is challenged to find the subject, the reader might as well give up all hope. Some punctuation helps.

```
If, while these toxic substances are
being transported by rail, the tanker
car positive seal filler and inspec-
tion hatch should be inadvertently
left unsecured, allowing atmospheric
moisture to commingle with the con-
tained substances, reaction of the
toxins with the moisture may result
in the escape into the atmosphere of
toxin-bearing mists.
```

A better solution, when time permits, is to rewrite to make punctuation less necessary.

```
Be sure that the tanker car's filler and inspection hatches
are tightly sealed. Otherwise, toxins may react with atmo-
spheric moisture and escape.
```

Don't, if you can help it, tolerate sentences, or other word groups, with lots of after-thoughts, rephrasings, and metadiscourse, all presented in short jerks, like this sentence. That's a common fault of copy that has gone through a chain of supervision, each link adding a new idea. Always try to have sentences that are written in a logical sequence and are as smooth as this one.

But again, if you need punctuation, don't hesitate to use it. It can make muddy sentences clear.

## CREATIVE PUNCTUATION

Most of us think of punctuation rules as being rigid. But actually, punctuation offers great opportunity to express ourselves creatively if we realize that our purpose is not to maintain "consistency" but to communicate freely and enthusiastically.

Technical editors use a lot of commas. In fact, one of the ways one can tell if a manuscript has been through a professional editor is to look for the commas.

"The comma has many uses, and is highly flexible," says *The Oxford Companion to the English Language* (1992). In technical writing, one of its chief uses is before the conjunction in a series, as in "a, b, and c." You may remember that in grade school teachers were divided about this usage, some saying that the *and* or *or* "takes the place of a comma."

Newspapers generally omit that comma, but in technical writing the consensus seems to be that it is necessary, because it aids readability by clearly separating the elements, especially when one of these elements has an internal *and*, like *research and development*.

## THE TROUBLE WITH RIGIDITY

There is general uniformity among editors and teachers about uses of the comma: between items in a list or parallel adjectives, to set off appositions, to separate clauses, to introduce direct speech, etc. However, there is not complete consistency.

Teachers may have to be more rigid than editors. To give a simple example, they may specify a comma after an introductory propositional phrase. But editors often omit this comma after a phrase like "In 1992 . . ." and then in the very next sentence turn around and put one in: "However, by 1993, . . . ."

In short, a teacher is indeed compelled to follow consistency. But an experienced editor has much more freedom.

Actually, the punctuation rules themselves tend to be flexible. A good grammar book will specify, "A comma *may* be used in introductory prepositional phrases," or "A comma *may* be used between two independent clauses." [Emphasis added.] This option is well worth preserving.

Frequently, an editor may want to omit the commas in a sentence that is getting too crowded with punctuation:

```
However, in 1993, for no reason, except, perhaps, rising
price-to-earnings ratios, investors, who heeded their in-
stincts, began a cautious retreat.
```

This is an example of an author's self-interruption, as discussed in Chapter 6, "Sentences." A good editor will clear most commas out, leaving:

```
However in 1993 for no reason except perhaps rising price-
to-earnings ratios, investors who heeded their instincts
began a cautious retreat.
```

One major comma remains, the one that divides the two major sections. Now the editor can decide which commas to return. That decision depends greatly on which element needs emphasis. The editor might put a pair around *in 1993*. Note the powerful influence that commas could have around *perhaps*. The seemingly insignificant comma carries a lot of punch.

Commas can also change a writer's meaning. There is a classic difference between "investors who heeded their instincts" and "investors, who heeded their instincts"; the latter phrase includes all investors and the former leaves some of them out. It's the difference between nonrestrictive and restrictive modifiers.

The rules are clear; commas go with the nonrestrictive construction. But in making the choice, an editor sometimes has to make a hairline distinction.

## RELAX THE RULES

In punctuation there is a tendency to try to make rules rigid, for "consistency."

Therefore, spurious rules are showing up in some textbooks, like "Do not use a comma before a trailing dependent clause." This works well in a sentence like "I like writers whose poems are graceful" but not at all well in "I like Keats, whose poems are graceful." The comma is needed because the clause is nonrestrictive.

Within the rules, commas are also governed by the length of the word group. For example, introductory prepositional phases may not be set off if they are short. Similarly, compound sentences do not require a comma if they are short enough, like "It snowed and we stayed home."

Even without a rule to guide her, an editor may want to insert a comma just to separate elements in a sentence, like "Keyboarders are required, to finish the work." Such commas are never illegal.

Editors definitely need to follow rules of punctuation, but they also need to know when to break them.

## ONE CONTROVERSIAL SOLUTION

Most of us grew up hearing teachers condemn that old rule-of-thumb, "Use a comma whenever you pause." We all know that this "rule" is not entirely reliable. When we say "the cozy, vine-covered cottage," most of us would make two pauses, after "cozy" and "vine-covered," but would use only one comma.

However, that rule-of-thumb may not be so bad after all. As Walter J. Ong (1944) of St. Louis University points out, the comma was invented in medieval times for that very purpose: to indicate a pause. So now, when editors are undecided, they could do worse than to ask, "Would I pause?" and punctuate accordingly.

## HYPHENS

Perhaps the second biggest punctuation problem is hyphens. Technical editors have a particular dilemma because they are caught in the middle between the engineers, who hate hyphens, and the keyboarders, who view them as an essential part of "the rules."

The big problem is the unit modifier (or unit-modifer) rule, which technical editors seldom follow, but which specifies that a modifier consisting of two words or more should be hyphened.

✍

> **"If you take hyphens seriously, you will surely go mad."**
> —John Benbow

Hyphens are often compared to measles, and company-style-manual compilers may be carriers. But, unlike the *Wall Street Journal,* technical authors are not likely to use wind-tunnel test, dry-cell battery, high-school graduate, third-base umpire, ice-cream cone, or 8-in-diameter-by-10-ft-length pipe.

Newspapers often follow the unit-modifier rule, but most technical documents do not. This may be because the documents spawn so many more compound adjectives. For example, a recent technical newsletter freely used an open style on "nose barrel extension," "work release order," "night attack capabilities," "performance appraisal form," and "merit review process." This didn't seem to offend their technical writing sensibilities.

Our readers' sensibilities, however, may be another matter. If there's any chance the readers won't understand long noun-string modifiers, it's probably best to unscramble them. Hyphenation often doesn't help, because of the way clauses are embedded. (See Chapter 6, "Sentences with Style," and Chapter 8, "Grammar.")

Most style manuals have lists of common compounds. But hyphens are most needed in "temporary compounds" that are not common. For example, a recent *Wall Street Journal* headline about a Russian pretender poked fun at "Used-Czar Shopping." *Used car* is a common modifier and may not need a hyphen (*used car lot, used car salesman*), but *used-czar,* tovarich, demands one.

Some words are nearly always hyphened, like *self-winding clock* or *low-pressure system*. Hyphens are ordinarily not needed for *high school teachers, structural dynamics problems,* or *technical writing practitioners.* Occasionally, however, you run into one like *bleed-air orifice* or *gust-front conditions* that is unusual enough that a simple hyphen is needed for clarity.

## COMPOUND NOUNS

Some compound nouns are hyphened also. They tend to follow fashion. Here are a few examples from *Compounding in the English Language,* by Alice Morton Ball (1939), who hunted hyphens in the Webster dictionaries of 1828, 1879, 1890, 1913, and 1934.

> In 1879, hyphens were in their heyday, with apple-tree, beef-eater, book-case, book-keeper, brides-maid, bullet-proof, chafing-dish, chicken-hearted, Christmas-day (now Christmas Day), counting-room, country-woman (but countryman), drawing-room, ebb-tide, fellow-citizen, fire-ball, fire-engine, foot-ball, good-will, high-priest, laughing-stock, life-blood, life-time, longshore-man, master-stroke, merry-making, non-essential, note-book, paper-weight, post-office, rolling-pin, safe-keeping, savings-bank, shell-fish, steam-boat, steam-engine, stepping-stone, text-book, to-day, walking-stick, water-mark, wrong-doer, and yellow-hammer.

This hyper-hyphenation largely stopped in the new dictionary of 1890. "It will be observed," that volume said,

> that the hyphen is less frequently used than in former editions. . . . The practice of lexicographers, authors, and printers is so various in this matter that in a multitude of instances it is hypercritical or whimsical to pronounce dogmatically that either the use or the omission of the hyphen is the only correct form.

This liberal statement bothered Horace Teall, writing in *The Compounding of English Words* (1891). He suggested using hyphens after nouns that were used attributively (*brick-yard*) but not after true adjectives (*brick house*). (He noted the heavy accent on the former, and viewed that as a discriminator.) He thus embraced hyphens in *book-shelves* and *thunder-cloud,* which have since become one word, and also in *freight-train, apple-tree, entrance-hall,* and *cider-mill,* which have not.

One modern-day technical editor hit upon this same solution recently, but ran into the wrenching problem of having to give a hyphen to *steel-guitar players* while denying it to *French horn virtuosi.*

To add to the hyphenation problem, English has many compound verbs, like *heat-treat, hard-boil,* and *keel-haul,* which legitimately take a hyphen, but only in their verb form (*ice-skate*).

Why didn't King Alfred straighten all this out once and for all?

To quote John Benbow, editor of the stylebook of the Oxford University Press, "If you take hyphens seriously, you will surely go mad." (Quoted in the *Harper Dictionary of Contemporary Usage,* 1975.)

## THE TREND TOWARD COMBINING WORDS

Many hyphened words do evolve into one word (motor-cycle, hand-kerchief). This is happening a lot in modern-day stylemanuals, e.g., online (adj.), copyedit (v.), database (n.), nonmilitary (adj.), desktop (n. or adj.), spreadsheet (n.), freshwater (adj.), and (yes) explosiveproof (adj.), evidently to be consistent with fireproof. Combining has also become fashionable in trade names (WordPerfect, FastLabel).

But nothing is new. Some notorious combining was practiced in *Philology on the English Language* by Richard Paul Jodrell (1820). Jodrell used, among others, fellowcandidate, foundlinghospital, pulpitsophistry, camelswallowing, and phantomnation, the latter taken from "phantom nation" in Alexander Pope's *Odyssey*.

According to William S. Walsh in his *Handy-Book of Literary Curiosities* (1911), some early lexicographer, in "foraging around for new words," struck "phantomnation" and assumed it to be Pope's. "Printers do not follow copy, sheep do not follow their leader, more closely than one lexicographer used to follow another," Walsh wrote. So the mistake got into *Worcester's Dictionary* (1859), the *Imperial Dictionary*, and also *Webster's* (around 1864), where, although labeled a "ghost word," it stayed until 1961.

In general, technical editors will find that confusion is lessened and text is made more readable if words are kept separate rather than being combined.

## CAPITALIZATION

Seekers of editorial consistency possibly find their greatest problem in capitalization. It's pretty well established that NASA's shuttle is lower-cased, although in some documents the Booster and the Orbiter may not be. What is an editor to do?

Some style manuals solve the problem simply by proclaiming solemnly, "Capitalize all proper nouns." Others try to have it both ways, claiming to follow the more professional "down" style while proceeding to capitalize everything in sight: titles, departments, committees, and hardware.

The editor of a style manual has a dilemma. Newspapers use a down style, which means that they do not capitalize, for instance, *manager* or *maintainability*. But managers like to have their titles capitalized, and the maintainability department turns purple if people don't capitalize Maintainability and even put a dash under the capital M.

In industrial writing, much of the capitalization is established by fiat, and the trend is all one way: *my* title, *my* department, *my* committee must be capitalized.

Most technical editors become tolerant of this attitude and have come to realize that capital letters are not all bad.

We say that we capitalize "major systems," but we do the opposite. We lower-case *computer*, or *monitor*, or *surge protector*, but we capitalize *Retaining Nut PN 647-98*. Why?

This seeming irrationality occurs because it is not importance that imposes capitals, it is uniqueness. We capitalize *the only* Society for Technical Communication, *the only* Government Printing Office, *the only* University of Chicago.

But what about John Smith? He is capitalized, but he is certainly not alone in that name. Nevertheless, he was given that appellation arbitrarily, uniquely, and distinctively, and not because he had any qualities of any other John Smith.

This is the custom, passed down to us by John Locke in the seventeenth century. Proper nouns denote, common nouns connote. We call something a tree because it is in a class of things that are all alike. A book, a desk, a surge protector are all common nouns, because they are named for their attributes. In contrast, given names are bestowed arbitrarily: John, Mary, and Heather Smith.

Editors can turn this built-in characteristic of language into an advantage.

Sometimes, in our reports, we have difficulty with semantics. We call something a "goal," and it soon gets lost among all the other goals we are also trying to achieve. So, to keep it from getting ignored, we give it a name, arbitrarily, and capitalize it. We can't call it the "John W. Smith Memorial Objective" without causing people to snicker, but we can christen it "Baseline Objective" or "Cumulative Objective." (Cumulative is a popular first name for progeny.)

Of course, in order to make a mark that is truly indelible, we instinctively know that we have to give our goal three names, like "Cumulative Multicultural Objective." Any new parent would be proud of a son like that, yes?

This trick works.

Of course, we don't really need capital letters as much as we think we do. But occasionally, capitalization can be useful to separate the wheat from the Cream of Wheat. Our present inconsistent practices actually make more sense than we sometimes think.

The main thing editors need to remember is that, compared to accuracy and clarity, capitalization is really minor. Be logical, be careful, be consistent. But as an editor, don't overkill the problem and let it distract you from attending to the important factors in the technical information.

# CHAPTER

## 10

## Editing Graphics

One of the distinguishing characteristics of technical writing is extensive use of graphs, charts, and tables. Illustrations are used to clarify complex information, emphasize facts, add coherence, summarize, and add interest.

In technical reports, graphics and layout add to the message. Engineers are sometimes scornful of graphic artists as people who want to "put rosettes in the corners." But artists are not there to make the book look pretty; they have an important function in reaching the reader. They add to the flow of the exposition and aid greatly in creating emphasis.

This whole philosophy is expressed well by Jan V. White in *Editing by Design* (1982). "There's more to creative magazine editing than marking up copy," White says at the start of his book. "By an aware use of expressive graphic elements, and a purposeful relationship of words, pictures, and space, design becomes communication, not mere ornament."

It used to be that in a professional organization the editor really didn't have much to do with graphics and production. That was left to the experts, people who were skilled in typing, printing, and illustration.

But in the modern day of desktop publishing, there is sometimes no one else to do it; the editor gets the job by default. It's perhaps unfortunate that some editors accept the job with eager enthusiasm and apply to it a rampant experimentation that is distinguished by its "variety" and "originality" rather than by its communicativeness and practical service to the reader.

You can't be against creativity, but creativity means more than just being "different." Besides, the more some editors try to be different, the more they produce documents that are the same.

Too many technical reports are cluttered and distracting, displaying art indiscriminately and smothering key messages. Proposals, understandably, are the worst. Typical artwork includes enormous flowcharts, with swirling labeled arrows pointing in all directions like falling leaves, crowding the edges of the page and creating an atmosphere of chaos akin to the proposal process itself.

In technical writing the important thing is the message, and all elements work together in its facile communication. The artwork and layout must be orderly, regular, and clean, with plenty of white space, readable typography, and short, pertinent headings.

## DOCUMENT DESIGN

In most technical reports, graphs and charts are intended to be distinctly functional, rather than decorative. Thus, like text, they all need editing.

If an author uses graphics, he should plan them right away, as part of his original organization. Proposals, for instance, should be 50 percent art. (See Appendix B, "Editing Technical Proposals.")Thus, it's a good idea to plan the artwork first and work the text around it, especially because art is a long-lead-time item. This does not mean, of course, that graphics should dominate the writing or take its place.

Often, the editor and the artist together can help the author look for possibilities for improving communication. They should look for candidates such as (1) complex information that visual presentation can make clearer, (2) information that is too detailed to be covered in words, and (3) information that deserves special emphasis.

## TYPES OF GRAPHICS

The old graphics standby is the line graph, or "mountain graph" (Figure 10.1), with values plotted along the ordinate (vertical) and the abscissa (horizontal). A line graph can take many forms, such as a scatter graph (Figure 10.2).

A bar graph (Figure 10.3) is good for comparing values; turned on its side, it becomes a schedule (Figure 10.4). A pie chart (Figure 10.5) is good for only one thing: comparing parts of a whole. Quite often editors can suggest inventive versions of these basic forms that clarify concepts and emphasize salient characteristics.

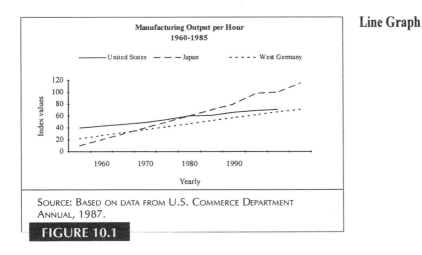

**Line Graph**

SOURCE: BASED ON DATA FROM U.S. COMMERCE DEPARTMENT ANNUAL, 1987.

**FIGURE 10.1**

**Scatter Graph**

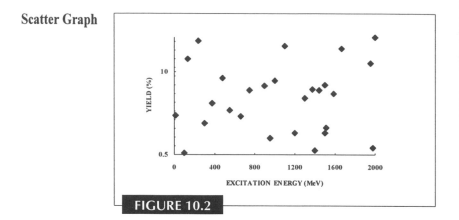

FIGURE 10.2

**Bar Chart**

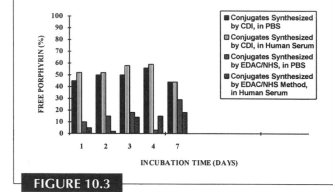

FIGURE 10.3

**Schedule**

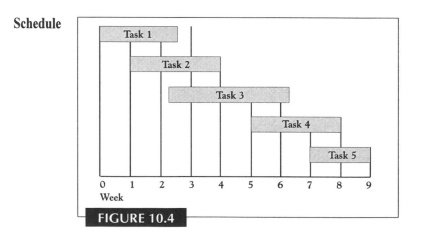

FIGURE 10.4

You can use other types of graphs for specific purposes, such as organization charts (Figure 10.6), block diagrams (Figure 10.7), wiring schematics (Figure 10.8), and various types of flow charts (Figure 10.9).

**Pie Chart**

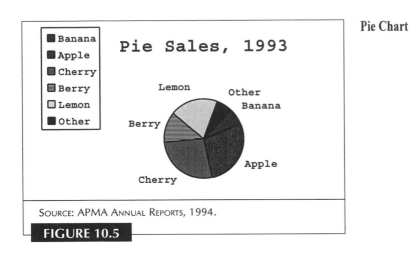

SOURCE: APMA ANNUAL REPORTS, 1994.

**FIGURE 10.5**

**Organization Chart**

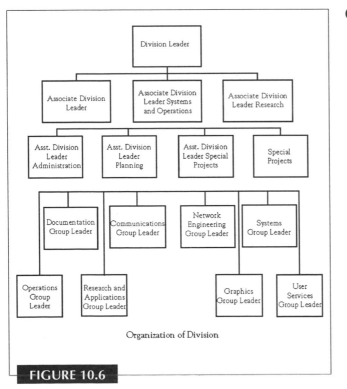

Organization of Division

**FIGURE 10.6**

As we say, charts have to be edited. Sometimes an author crams unrelated comparisons onto the same line graph, with multiple scales, "to save space." At other times he may try unsuccessfully to draw a bar graph comparing $7500, $150, $10, and $1.98 (see Figure 10.10), when two charts would have been better (one comparing $7500 with "all others" and another comparing the others).

A graph is a visual device. What the viewer sees is what counts. That means it is senseless to shorten a bar by cutting the middle out and labelling it "$7500" (Figure 10.10).

Except in rare cases, all scales should start at zero to avoid distortion, and steer away from unusual divisions like "0, 3.5, 7, 10.5. . . ." Similarly, avoid logarithmic scales except in special cases—measuring earthquakes (Richter scale), tracking decibels or high-energy electrical charges (Figure 10.2), or using a descendant of the old slide rule.

**Block Diagram**

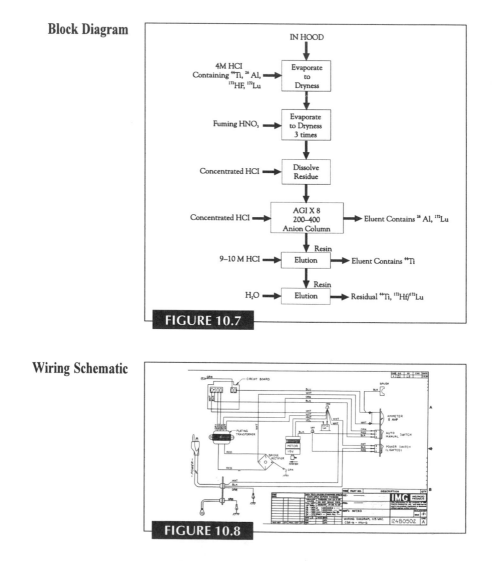

**Wiring Schematic**

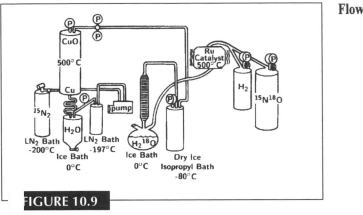

**Flow Diagram**

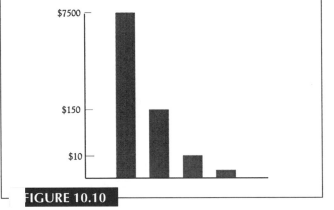

**Bad Practice:
Awkward Scale**

Also, use the left and bottom for your axes. All this helps the reader tell at a glance what's going on.

When working with a vertical 8½ x 11 in. page, use a vertical format so the reader won't have to turn the book around. He probably won't do it!

Since figures are frequently borrowed, the source of the data they contain should go in a source line below the caption. It's not wise to list sources in the bibliography and expect readers to look up that source before they "borrow" the figure to use in a document of their own. It's much better to have the source indicated on the figure itself. (See Figures 10.1, 10.5, and 10.12.)

## ENVISIONING INFORMATION

Above all, keep graphs simple. One clear word is worth a thousand cluttered pictures. Artwork variety too often becomes artwork confusion. Simplicity is effective.

Avoid clutter of all types. This includes the "chartjunk" so eloquently demonstrated by Edward R. Tufte in his two splendid books, *The Visual Display of Quantitative Information* (1984) and *Envisioning Information* (1990). Minimize the scales in the margin, and especially avoid those rosettes in the corners. Make the image itself stand out.

Tufte points out that graphics were not invented until the latter half of the eighteenth century. But now, modern datagraphics are instruments for reasoning about quantitative information. Often the most effective way to explore a set of numbers is to look at pictures of those numbers. His second book shows how artists can escape from the "flatland" of the printed page to make those explorations more vivid.

In all your artwork, use common sense. For example, make your shading match your numbers. If you have a U. S. map showing production of soybeans by state, make the heavy producers dark and the light ones light. Mixing up patterns confuses the reader. The object of any artwork is to help the reader comprehend quickly.

## PHOTOGRAPHS

In proposals, manuals, and technical reports, don't forget the advantages of photographs. Select good photos, clear photos, photos that show something. Crop them heavily, to move in close to the subject and get just what you want. Find pictures with a single center of interest and as few people gathered around as possible.

Use pictures with people doing something. This may mean showing a slightly cluttered desk, a turned shoulder, a pencil behind an ear (instead of pointing at something). Most industrial pictures seem so posed that the caption might well read, "John Smith is shown having his picture taken."

Pick pictures that use patterns, repetition, shadows, silhouettes, motion, "fuzzy" focus, unusual angles. Watch your backgrounds. Use art group techniques to cut clutter.

Art is secondary to function, but there is no harm in making the function visually appealing, as long as your message remains clear! For instance, in your layout, vary the size of your pictures to add interest. Don't blow up the pictures that are "pretty," but rather those that best tell your readers the story.

Jan White has some interesting ideas about using a common feature, like a horizon, to unify a series of pictures, and about sustaining interest by placing similar art at the same location on successive pages.

## ACTION CAPTIONS

An editor can help pictures with good captions. Don't say, "John Smith is shown hanging a picture." That's obvious; John's the one with the hammer. Save your words to give details about why the picture is being hung.

Most of the time, particularly on proposals, you will want to use "action captions." Instead of saying "Take-off distance vs. weight," you can point out that "The Model 199 takes off in 1500 ft." The inherent danger in action captions, of course, is that they can get too salesy and bombastic, thereby negating their effect.

Don't try to tell two stories, one in the picture and one in the caption. And don't combine captions for several pictures in a single copy block. That's a sure sign that the editor is trying to help the layout, not the reader.

Use the captions to sharpen the image of the picture, and the picture to enhance the message of the document.

Keep captions and headings short: "Short enough to be interesting but long enough to cover the subject." Let your artwork speak out. Provide only enough words to simplify, not to elaborate. Refer the reader to a graph and the one point it illustrates; don't belabor the details.

In a long text illustrated by a large diagram, call the figure out early. Don't make the reader wade through a long written explanation without the benefit of the visual guide.

## FIGURE NUMBERS

It is conventional to put figure numbers (and the captions) on the bottom of the item, but table numbers and captions on the top, close to the column headings (Figure 10.11).

**Sample Table**

### Table 1
### Survey Respondents by Region

| Region | Total Responses | Valid Responses | Favoring Alternative 1 | Favoring Alternative 2 |
|---|---|---|---|---|
| Northeast | 847 | 821 | 653 | 166 |
| Southeast | 635 | 618 | 237 | 381 |
| Midwest | 723 | 717 | 320 | 397 |
| Southwest | 522 | 498 | 302 | 196 |
| Northwest | 605 | 593 | 375 | 218 |

**FIGURE 10.11**

Most companies nowadays, however, apply the term "figures" to both tables and figures (including charts, maps, schematics, photos, sketches, etc.) This prevents having to carry a double set of numbers, one perhaps being roman numerals. (Roman numerals are hard to read and awkward when reserving space for callouts. You have to reserve seven spaces, because any table might be XXXVIII.) This modern expediency not only simplifies production but also is less frustrating for the reader.

There are two options in numbering figures: (1) consecutively throughout or (2) by section or subsection. The smaller bites are easier to handle in case of changes, and it makes no difference to the reader. By the way, the reader doesn't mind if, in a proposal emergency, you have to skip a figure number or insert a "Figure 38a" at the last minute.

## INTEGRATING FIGURES

Integrate figure and tables with text as much as possible; don't put all the figures at the end of the book.

If possible, put each visual near its reference. From a reader's standpoint, putting all the visuals together at the back of a chapter or report is very bad practice. There was some excuse for doing this back in the days when the art and the text were prepared separately and not integrated until the last minute, but even then the graphics should have been put on the page following their references whenever possible.

There is one principal rule: the callout obviously must precede the figure (except for a frontispiece, of course). But try to get the figure on the same page as its callout; then the reader can look at the figure while he is reading the text, without flipping back and forth. Now, when almost everyone works with full-featured word processors or page-layout programs, it is easier to put the graphic on the same page as its reference.

Nevertheless, this convenience is sometimes hard to manage. If a callout falls at the bottom of a page and there is not enough room for the figure, it must go at the top of the next one. Then the following callout goes on the bottom half of that page and the accompanying figure at the top of the next, etc. Thus, all callouts begin to fall on different pages from the art they call out.

The way to break this dismal pattern is to lay out each section backwards. Then, no matter where the figure is located, there will probably be room for the small callout on the same page.

There is really only one disadvantage to this technique: you have to find something to fill the leftover space that now, instead of going at the end, falls on page 1.

If you can't get your computer to run backwards, simply try to put your figures at the bottom of the pages, to leave room for the callouts. Some people imagine that pictures should go at or near the top of the page, as in an art gallery, but in technical reports, putting pictures below their callouts favors the reader.

## COLOR

What about color? In its place it is invaluable. It's one more tool in the wide variety of art techniques that can supplement writing. It can be used to decorate, to emphasize, or to unify.

But also, color adds a great deal of expense and time. It tends to make a document look as though the editors squandered money. Indiscriminate color, too, can become "scarlet fever."

Jan White maintains that color is not half as important to the reader as to the editor. The reader sees a lot of color in ads, and, becoming jaded, tends to overlook it in editorial matter.

"The editor, on the other hand," he says, "rarely gets the opportunity to use color. He or she thinks its rarity makes it wonderful—ascribes all sorts of marvelous capabilities to it. Alas, by itself it won't fly anywhere."

Color, White says, should be controlled intellectually, not emotionally. This topic he covers in a separate book called *Color for the Electronic Age* (1990).

## TYPOGRAPHY

Please don't be tempted by the exotic typefaces available in your new desktop publishing software. They complicate communications, rather than simplify them.

Artists tend to agree that the most attractive books result from using the same family of type throughout, rather than seeking "variety" by mixing serif and sans-serif, curved and straight, stolid and graceful. Type families have plenty of variety within themselves: large and small, bold and light, condensed and extended, roman and italic. The result is variety without loss of an appealing, gracious unity.

Remember, though, that if you have something important to say, do not put it into italics. Italics are hard to read. Save them for captions and short headings. Similarly, boldface is too often overused, especially on proposals. It shouts at the reader, like an over-loud TV commercial.

For readability, choose standard type with serifs. Those without serifs, like Futura, Helvetica, or Gothic, are extremely popular at this writing, but they are not nearly as easy to read as even the venerable Century Schoolbook font (as you know if you have tried to read the TV book without your glasses). Sans-serif type has its uses, but it should be confined to short copy.

If you want to indulge your artistic urge to do something different, pick a graceful type with long ascenders and descenders rather than the "machine type" favored in word processors. Be aware, though, that graceful type does have one disadvantage: It looks smaller. That's because, with its long tails, it obviously has a smaller "x-height" (the height of the lower-case "x" in that font).

Type is commonly measured in points, a point being 1/12 of a pica and a pica 1/6 of an inch. (Book type is commonly around 10–11 points.) But "x-height" is a better absolute measure for readability.

X-height can be used to substantiate the tested "unreadability" of all-caps. If a *D* were reduced so its x-height was the same as a *d*, it would be much less readable than *d*, especially if it was in a line with many *O's, Q's*, and *B's*. And in most fonts, the lower case and small caps would take about the same space.

Watch the widths of your columns. Repeated tests have shown that the ideal column is about 39–40 characters, or "an alphabet and a half." Narrower columns create awkward spacing and wider ones cause some readers problems in tracking from line to line, and therefore require more leading.

You may be surprised that in technical reports a two-column format may save space, despite the alley down the middle. This is because the columns are narrower and you waste less space with every blank line, title, or widow.

Beware of dark paper. Instead, make your type dark and your paper pastel. A background of burnished gold or throbbing mauve may look great in a painting, but readers' eyes need contrast. A bright blue printed on a bright red is hard to see. In fact, if you want your message to be read, you can't beat black on white.

One seeming contradiction. On slides to be shown in a darkened room, a pastel (not white) on black seems to be easier on viewers' eyes, partly because it minimizes changes in the room's light level.

## WHITE SPACE

In technical reports you can often create marvelous effects by using lots of nothing at all—namely, white space. Perhaps this is true because white space is used so rarely. Engineers and technical writers alike have the urge to fill up every inch with copy (no matter how bad the copy may be). They do not realize how much the white space contributes in the way of order and clarity as well as attractiveness and repose.

If you are ever asked to produce a truly elegant brochure, don't use color and headlines; try instead a graceful serif type with long ascenders and descenders on an expensive off-white stock with plenty of white space. Instead of looking like a magazine ad, your creation will seem like an announcement of an important, happy occasion.

## COMPUTERS AND GRAPHICS

It is vital today to have access to computer hardware for word processing, spreadsheets, and desktop publishing.

Word processing software is primarily used for typing words, although many programs also have provisions for drawing. It can help a writer (or editor) review and edit, using commands to *insert/delete, move, copy,* and *search and replace.* Other features may include spell checkers, electronic thesauri, and grammar and style checkers.

Spreadsheets can provide copy, including numbers, in columns and rows. They can also help create line charts, bar charts, pie charts, and other graphic devices.

Desktop publishing software is useful for newsletters, long reports, manuals, and proposals. This software combines text and graphics into complete page designs.

Other graphics software available includes clip art, or ready-to-use pictures of various subjects (Figure 10.12); programs to help create elementary drawings (Figure 10.13); scanners that read a picture and convert it into digital format (Figure 10.14). Advanced programs are also available to create precise engineering drawings, even in three dimensions, and can be combined with machine tooling (CAD/CAM) to create parts automatically.

There are many exotic graphics applications used in multi-media presentations, several of which rival film companies for sophistication. In addition to basic graph and chart capabilities, they can present special effects like fading, wiping, scrolling, and spiraling. However, these programs can cost as much as $50,000, and require the expertise of professional graphic designers.

Two excellent books on computers and art are William K. Horton's *Designing and Writing Online Documentation* (1990) and *Illustrating Computer Documentation* (1991). In the latter book, Horton has a cogent criticism for all of us about "failing to edit graphics—tolerating shoddy, even misleading, graphics while sweating over a comma that only an editor would notice."

**Example of Clip Art**

SOURCE: WORD PERFECT 6.0 [COYOTE.WPG]

FIGURE 10.12

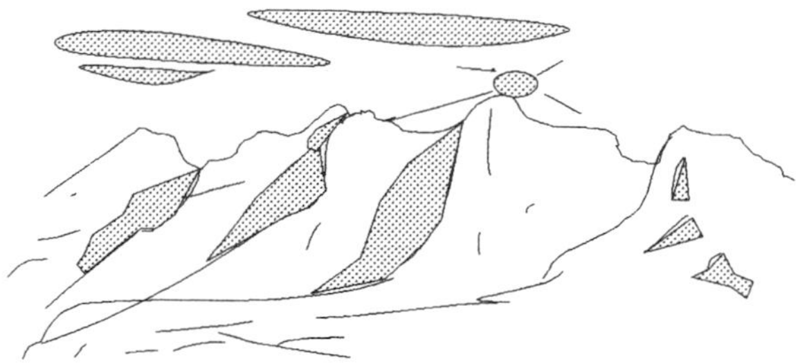

**Simple Line Drawing Done with Computer Graphics Program**
(WPDraw)

FIGURE 10.13

## COST CONTROL

Editors, especially in industry, have at least two audiences: the readers of the document and the people who are paying the bill.

Most of the time, conscientious editors are rightly on the side of the reader. But they obviously can't ignore the wishes of their bosses, and when production costs rise dramatically, editors can get in trouble.

Image Digitized from
Photo by Scanner

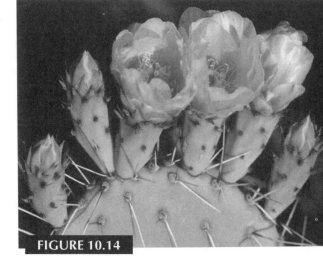

FIGURE 10.14

Editors often push for larger publications, with more art, fancier covers, heavier paper, and especially, as noted above by Jan White, more color. But such embellishments do not always have the desired effect.

One story is told about the division of a major company that tried to impress the company president by issuing its own four-color, slick paper "annual report." They presented it proudly to the top man, but the recipient growled, "How much did this cost?"

That was the last annual report published by that division.

If you are working for a public institution, like a public utility, a social agency, or a political party, then your readership may well object to fancy covers, for the simple reason that they feel like they are paying the bill.

So the lesson offered by top public relations experts about reports and brochures is to "make them look cheap." Spend your money, they say, on good writing, good paper and design, and white space, but never on flamboyance.

Nowadays in technical writing, opportunities for economy are legion, not only in brochures but in technical manuals. As discussed in Appendix A, "Editing Technical Manuals," many documents are too large, and in some cases may not even be needed. The wisest editor may be the one who works on ways to save company money by downsizing the routine regurgitation and accentuating ways either to provide necessary information more cheaply or to eliminate the need for that information entirely.

# CHAPTER

**11**

# Marking Manuscripts

Traditionally, manuscript marking has been the characteristic feature of the editor's trade. *Manuscript* originally meant *handwritten* (Latin *manus*, hand), but the word has become more or less synonymous with *typescript*. In either case, there is a physical sheet on which an editor can make marks with a hand-held implement. When an editor makes a change, it is visible—editors usually use bright-colored inks.

The words *marking* and *manuscript* have taken on new meaning as word processors have become the standard tools of the trade. When the physical form of a document is a file consisting of binary code on magnetic media, anybody who has access to the file can change it—and no one may be able to tell. These files, perhaps, should be called *computerscripts* to distinguish them from their ancestors, although we continue to call the hardcopy output of a computerscript a "typescript."

Most word processors contain features that make it possible to edit visibly—for example, using text boxes for queries, using strikeout to indicate copy to be cut, or coloring inserted passages. There are also software products that compare old and new versions of a typescript, highlighting the alterations. According to conversations on Copyediting-L, the Internet conference (May 1994), such software works pretty well for both editors and authors.

Nevertheless, editing continues to be done by marking on paper printouts. Why?

A one-word answer: accountability. When marked-up copy is available, authors can more easily see what changes editors have recommended. Also, despite advances in video-monitor technology, hardcopy is easier to read. Most monitors show only about one-half page at a time.

Accountability also works to the editor's advantage. Unless people (particularly managers) can actually see what editors do, editors' contributions may remain unacknowledged—a definite disadvantage at review time. And sometimes editors' recommendations, though better than the authors', are overridden. A marked-up typescript becomes an insurance policy.

So, even though the demise of paper has been predicted for 30 years, editors should learn standard copyediting marks.

## EDITORS' MARKS AND PROOFREADERS' MARKS

Some corporate style guides don't distinguish between editors' and proofreaders' marks. *The Chicago Manual of Style,* 14th ed., discusses the two separately, but there are obvious similarities. That's because both sets of marks were originally intended for communicating with typesetters, to whom the marks have definite and well-known meanings. If you have to communicate with typesetters about setting manuscripts in type or about correcting galley proofs, you should definitely be able to use the appropriate marks.

However, it's becoming ever more rare for printed material to be keyboarded at a printshop. Material that is to be typeset is usually submitted in coded electronic formats, the keyboarding already done.

Editors, then, are marking typescripts mostly for keyboarders who are not linotype operators, or for authors who may have keyboarded their own drafts.

In some cases, the editor may be responsible for having the rekeyboarding done; in other cases, it will be done by a third party.

## LANGUAGE-EDITING MARKS

The most-used marks for language editing are insertion, deletion, transposition, and sequence. Insertion is usually indicated by a caret (^), deletion by a long line with a curly tail (see Example 11.1), transposition by a horizontal $S$ (∽) with each bulge encompassing the words to be transposed, and sequence by horizontal parentheses or a simple line drawn to the next word in a sequence.

If editors were marking up typescripts so they could later change the computerscripts, they could use a shorthand intelligible only to themselves. But since they are more often working with people who aren't compositors, they need to use marks that are either well known or intuitively obvious.

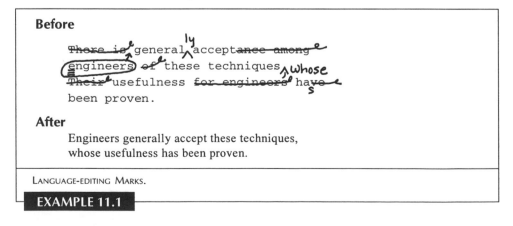

**Before**

After

        Engineers generally accept these techniques,
        whose usefulness has been proven.

LANGUAGE-EDITING MARKS.

**EXAMPLE 11.1**

Example 11.2 shows marking for a content edit. The marking chops three paragraphs, indicating where to move them. It also changes the style of a heading from a main head to a secondary head, and it inserts copy to make a point clearer.

A better solution, when time permits ✗ is to:
¶ Rewrite to make punctuation inherently unnecessary.
   Be sure that the tanker car's filler and inspection hatch are tightly sealed. Otherwise toxins may escape. ~react with atmospheric moisture and,~
   Don't, if you can help it, tolerate sentences like this one with lots of afterthoughts, ^all presented in short jerks. That's ? a common fault of technical copy which has gone through a chain of supervision, each link adding a new idea. Always try to have sentences that are written in a logical sequence and are as smooth as this one. ?
   But again, if you need punctuation (Chapter 9), don't hesitate to use it. It can make muddy sentences clear.

*Put under punctuation*

EDITING FOR EMPHASIS  B head

Important as it is to cut out useless verbiage, it's not enough to create efficient sentences. Another law of editing, formulated by George Campbell, Scottish minister and author of *The Philosophy of Rhetoric* (1776), is this:
~Good sentences must have emphasis.~
**"For strength of sentences, never end them with an adverb, a preposition, or any inconsiderable word."**
We know that law; it has descended to us in a narrower form in our grammar books. It's good advice for editors, not because of what it prohibits about prepositions, but rather for what it says about the strength of the periodic sentence.
   You may have learned ^in grammar that English has two types of sentences: the loose sentence and the periodic sentence. The loose sentence starts with its main point and tails off. It is a sentence in which the main idea is completed before the sentence finishes.

COPY MARKED FOR CONTENT EDIT.

**EXAMPLE 11.2**

## MARKS THAT CHANGE TYPE CHARACTERISTICS

Other more specialized marks depend not on intuition, as do the marks in Example 11.2, but on the keyboarder's knowledge of marks that are in general use. Some change the characteristics of the type, as shown in Example 11.3. Note that a translation of each mark is provided in the left margin, enclosed in a circle, so that a keyboarder won't confuse it with text. Such circled translations may be necessary for keyboarders

| Marginal Note | Marked Copy | Intent of Marking |
|---|---|---|
| *bf* | Not all people | Not **all** people |
| *ital* | Not all people | Not *all* people |
| *stet* | Not all people | Not all people |
| *sm caps* | Not all people | Not ALL people |
| *all caps* | Not all people | Not ALL people |
| *init caps* | not all people | Not all people |
| *rom* | Not *all* people | Not all people |
| *U/lc* | NOT ALL PEOPLE | Not All People |

MARKS FOR CHANGING TYPE CHARACTERISTICS.

**EXAMPLE 11.3**

who aren't compositors. Even for compositors, according to Kimberley Eiland, who directs the Public Information Office at New Mexico Tech (Socorro), the circled instructions don't hurt. "I've never had a typesetter complain about directions that were redundantly clear," she says.

## MARKS THAT ALTER SPATIAL LAYOUT

Other marks change the spatial layout of the type by deleting and inserting space, by shifting text to the right or left, or by creating new paragraph breaks. Space marks are shown in Example 11.4.

The ¶ symbol means "paragraph" and can be used to call for a normal paragraph indention.

The □ symbol corresponds to an em-space. (An em-space is a space the width of the capital *M*, the widest character in a font.) If a number 5 is written in the box, it indicates a 5-em space, or, when drawn at the margin, it indicates a 5-em block indent. A □ with a diagonal line through it indicates an en-space (half an em), but most of us will have scant occasion to use it.

A # with its left vertical drawn between two letters means "insert a space"; it's usually used to separate two words erroneously run together.

A ⌐ line that looks like a squared "S" between words means to start the second word on a new line.

A ⌐ at the margin means to set the text flush to the left margin; similarly, a ¬ at the right margin means "set text flush right."

---

**Before**

At this point the sorter is ready for operation in either the automatic or the manual mode. Automatic mode. The digitally controlled table moves the radius translation table. Manual mode. Through the microscope the operator inspects each chip for physical integrity and reads the ink code. He then selects the control button that corresponds to the code.

Either mode should produce good results.

**After**

At this point the sorter is ready for operation in either the automatic or the manual mode.

**Automatic mode.** The digitally controlled table moves the radius translation table.
**Manual mode.** Through the microscope the operator inspects each chip for physical integrity and reads the ink code. He then selects the control button that corresponds to the code.

Either mode should produce good results.

Marks that Change Spatial Arrangement.

**EXAMPLE 11.4**

---

## MARKS THAT INSERT PUNCTUATION

You might think that inserting punctuation marks would be straightforward. The problem is, though, that standard copyediting symbols are not wholly intuitive. When you use the copyediting mark for inserting a hyphen, you may have an equals sign turn up in the typescript. Moral: know thy keyboarder.

The standard punctuation-editing marks are shown in Example 11.5. In Example 11.6, the marks are applied.

## MARKS USED IN PROOFREADING

Proofreading, as done in print shops of yore, was a painstaking activity. Since proofreaders were reading galley proofs, they had to use the marks we've already seen, plus a few others peculiar to the setting of metal type. Their work was confined mainly to catching typographical mistakes made by compositors and to noticing broken or misaligned type. They often worked in pairs, one person reading from the galley (punctuation and all) as the other read the original. Errors were noted with caret or other mark at the point of occurrence, and a notation was made in the margin so a compositor scanning the galleys could quickly find the places needing correction.

Galley-reading time was not—is not—a time to be editing text. Changes in galley are expensive.

As the transition from hard copy typescripts to computerscripts continues, proof-reading of the sort just described is ever more rare. In a manual or report that is desk-top-published, "proofreading" has become nearly synonymous with the screening edit, which doesn't require many of the traditional proofreaders' marks.

Some brochures or annual reports are sent to a printer, and if you are reading these galleys, you will need to use proofreaders' marks. If your printer doesn't supply a sheet that explains the marks, you should consult *The Chicago Manual of Style*; the *GPO Style Manual*; International Paper's *Pocket Pal: A Graphic Arts Production Handbook*; or the style manual that is standard for the field in which you are editing. (See Appendix C.)

| Mark | Symbol | Comment |
|------|--------|---------|
| Period | ⊙ | Draw a circle around a comma; period |
| Comma | ⋏ | Draw a hat and a tail on a period; comma |
| Colon | ⊙ | Two dots vertically in a circle |
| Semicolon | ⋏ | Dot over comma under hat |
| Apostrophe | ⋎ | Comma in a funnel over the line |
| Quotation Marks | ⋓ ⋓ | American: Two left- or right-facing commas in a funnel |
|  | ⋎ ⋎ | British: One left- or right-comma in a funnel |
| Hyphen | = | Looks like an "equals" sign |
| En-dash | ⊥N | Usually indicates a range |
| Em-dash | ⊥M | The more usual dash |
| Parentheses | ⧘ ⧙ | Note the marks that keep them distinct |
| Brackets | [ ] | Square, not rounded |
| Subscript | ∧ | Hat over letter or number |
| Superscript | ∨ | Letter or number captured in funnel |

MARKS FOR EDITING PUNCTUATION.

**EXAMPLE 11.5**

**Before**

Aqua regia—which in Latin means royal water—is a mixture
of nitric acid (HNO₃) and hydrochloric acid (HCl) it's the only
reagent that will dissolve gold and platinum, the noble
metals, hence, according to Abernathy 16, its association with
royalty.

**After**

Aqua regia—which in Latin means royal water—is a mixture of nitric acid ($HNO_3$) and
hydrochloric acid (HCl). It's the only reagent that will dissolve gold and platinum, the
noble metals; hence, according to Abernathy,[16] its association with royalty.

**EXAMPLE 11.6**

# CHAPTER

# 12

## Triage: Dealing with Typescripts under Deadline

**M**ore often than not, editors will not have enough time or budget to do everything a typescript needs. So, in order to save the entire document, they need guidelines to help them decide what editing can be neglected.

Editors are always under the gun. They are the ones who are squeezed between the procrastinations of the writers and the implacable needs of the printer. They seldom have enough time to do the job right, and almost never have the chance to do a job over.

Often, then, editors must enter the triage mode. They must sacrifice some editorial duties to save the entire document. The question is, what does an editor need to do most?

Most of all, the editor needs to read the copy and see if it makes sense. Even if she doesn't have time for much reorganization or copy cutting, she might be able to save the author embarrassment. After that, she can do minor chores like checking for consistency of capitalization.

Sometimes she can get the subject experts to check consistency, format the heads, check the figure numbers, and number the pages; they enjoy doing that kind of work, for a short while, and are nearly always happy to pitch in, now that their writing is done.

Nowadays, by the way, many routine editing jobs can be done by machine, freeing human editors for reading the copy.

Note that this approach to triage is almost the direct opposite of the routine implied by the "Levels of Edit," the system adapted from old costing procedures by the Jet Propulsion Labs, Pasadena, California. That system implies that reading the content is less urgent than checking the grammar, the table of contents, and the end-of-line hyphenation, and whether the titles of figures are outside the margins.

Of course, effective triage depends on many things:

1. **What kind of document it is.** For proposals, the detailed formatting is much less important than the content. For an annual report, the formatting may

---

**The JPL Levels of Edit**

Coordination (production expediting)
Policy (conforming to house style)
Integrity (making sure it's all there)
Screening (minimal language editing)
Copy clarification (for typesetter)
Format edit (headings, columns, etc.)
Mechanical style edit (consistency check)
Language edit (clarity, concession)
Substantive edit (logic, organization)

take precedence, but we would hope that an annual report would never have to go through triage anyway.

2. **The competence of the author.** If the text has been written by a professional writer or by an expert known for her organizational and writing ability, the editor can indeed work on checking figure numbers, typos, etc.

3. **The competence of the editor.** A good content editor can read up to 100 double-spaced pages a day, unless the copy is unusually muddy or full of mathematics. It therefore takes her less time, and she can do that before starting on the details.

4. **The status of the editor in the organization.** If editors are expected to pussy-foot and do only clerical tasks, then those duties might assume priority. If they are expected to help shape the accuracy and readability of the document, that's what they should do, even at the last minute. (By the way, editors should not be content to do clerical chores when there are so many opportunities for good copy-revisers.)

5. **The audience.** If the report is designed for wide public distribution, then hordes of people from everywhere should perhaps be pulled in to check for consistency and typos. Typos are obviously less important on routine quarterly reports or on proposals, where the RFP itself is frequently replete with typos and inconsistencies.

6. **The need for obvious details.** A cover, a table of contents, page numbers— these indeed rank as priority items. Someone, sometime, should also check to see that the customer's name is not spelled wrong. It can indeed happen.

There are obviously a lot of tasks that can be left to the last, even though time may indeed run out. These include capitalization, hyphens, inconsistent use of numbers, the style of bibliographic references, letter spacing, and many others.

Where the "Levels of Edit" is particularly valuable is not in assigning tasks, but in costing work that has been done. If you ask an author if he wants a thorough edit or just a bindery check, he will opt for the latter, especially if he is a poor writer. Thus, the worst writers get the least editing.

There are important exceptions. Writers often welcome intelligent editing, to help catch their mistakes. Workers struggling with a sales brochure, a speech, or an important memo to the boss almost always welcome collaborative editing. Authors who are over their page limits almost demand editing, because they know that editors can "take things out without taking anything out."

When it gets right down to it, the depth of the editing depends almost entirely on the trust between author and editor.

## EXAMPLE: ENGINEERING PROPOSAL

To demonstrate triage in action, the following example displays an assignment actually given to an editor, showing the kinds of decisions that editors often have to make under deadline pressures. It involves a proposal prepared by an engineering firm.

(Names and locations have been changed.) Like most proposals, it contains both original prose, describing how the firm proposes to address the prospective client's problem, and boilerplate, descriptions of the firm's previous projects and of the related experience of the people whom the firm proposes to assign to the client's project.

The original editor was given about three hours to "fix it up" before the proposal went into final production. What would you do to it if you could, and what do you think you should do given only three hours? (Note: The proposal had no title page or table of contents; what the editor saw first is what you see first.)

THE FIRM

Rackstraw, Tucker and Associates, Inc. (RTA) is a small business enterprise incorporated in the Province of Graniola with orifices in Grand Cataract and Cloud City, Graniola. The firm has a staff of 21 engineers, technologist, and support personnel. RTA has provided professional engineering services to servile public and private clients throughout Graniola since 1975.

The three principles of RTA together, bring over 60 years of professional engineering experience and are Registered Professional engineers in the Province of Graniola and several other provinces. Mr. Ralph Rackstraw, is a registered land surveyor and professional engineer in the province of Graniola. With the addition of Mr. Joseph Porter as a Senior Consultant Transportation, the firm' s accumulated total staff experience now accedes 100 years.

The firm utilizes Computer Aided Design (CAD) on most of its projects and is equipped with numerous modern computer hardware and software in addition to state of the art survey instruments.

The firm' s clients include the G.P.H.&T.D. , the City of Grand Cataract, Marigold Township, Corneal Township, City of Cloud City, Becket Community Development Corporation, Horstgraben Land and Development Company, the Huh Aboriginal Nation, and numerous public and private clients throughout Graniola.

RTA carries general and professional liability insurance in units typical for engineering practices in Graniola.

The firm takes pride in aggressive project management and active involvement of the principals in project design, quality assurance, and construction administration.

Over eighty percent (80%) of the firm' s gross revenues come from repeat clients which speaks well of our reputation.

1.2 THE PRINIPALS:

Messrs Bill Bobstay, Ralph Rackstraw, and Tom Tucker are the three principals of the firm. All of the principals are registered professional engineers in the Province of

Graniola. Mr. Rackstraw is also a registered land surveyor in the Province of Graniola.

Each of the three principals actively participate in the design, quality assurance, construction phase, and project management of the firm's projects.

The Graniola registration number of the three principals are provided below:

Bill Bobstay, P.E. Graniola P. E. No. 14138

Ralph Rackstraw, P.E. , L.S. Graniola P.E. No. 15457

Tom Tucker, P.E. Graniola P. E. No. 14424

UNDERSTANDING OF THE SCOPE OF WORK:

Based on the meeting of April 22, 1994, the following reflects our understanding of the scope of services.

Cripps Chromium Corporation intends to conduct Chromium Mining operation at the Pinafore Mine within the Corcoran National Land Preserve in Corcoran Township, Graniola. Mining operation is anticipated to commence in 1996.

- Open pit type mining will be utilized. Pit dimensions are anticipated to be 2, 000 ft. x 2, 000 ft.
- Heap leach type operation is proposed at this time.
- Approximately 60 million tons of waste material will be generated during the operation. The waste material will include waste rock, tailings and spent ore.
- Blasting will be utilized.
- Current plans call for creation of a dam on Hebe Creek for stockpiling the ore.
- Major environmental concerns include existence of wilderness boundary near the sight.
- Leaching of processing chemicals into natural streams on groundwater.
- Impacts related to access and haul roads.
- All EIS activities must be coordinated with the Corcoran National Land Preserve Staff.
- Work will be preformed in accordance with the memorandum of understanding being executed between Cripps Chromium Corporation and the Bureau of Environmental Affairs, Corcoran National Land Preserve.
- Cripps Chromium Corporation wishes to retain specialty consultants such as archaeologists as independent contractors. RTA will be required to coordinate with these consultants and appropriately incorporate the data and information in the EIS.

The project manager will prepare an outline of the EIS document and obtain concurrence from the Bureau of Environmental Affairs.

The project manager will assign EIS study tests to the various team members commensurate with their respective area of expertise.

   The EIS will be prepared in accordance with BEA require-
ments. The elements of the document will include but not
necessarily be limited to the following environmental fac-
tors.
1. Land Resources:
   - Topography
   - Soil
   - Geology
   - Drainage and Erosion
   - Earthquakes and other natural disasters
2. Water Resources:
   - Surface and Ground Water quality
   - Use
   - Rights
3. Air Resources:
   - Quality
   - Permitting
4. Wild Life
5. Vegetation
6. Biological Ecosystem
7. Agriculture:
   - Crops
   - Livestock
8. Cultural Resources:
   - Historic
   - Religious
   - Archeological
9. Socio-Economic:
   - Employment
   - Attitude
   - Life Style
   - Local Tax base advantages
10. Resource Use:
   - Hunting
   - Fishing
   - Crop Harvesting
   - Mining
   - Recreation
   - Transportation
   - Other Land Use
11. Noise
12. Wilderness
13. Public Health and Safety

Each team member will evaluate environmental impacts for
his/her area of specialty. This evaluation will include the
following key elements.
-    Collection of historical data and background
-    Environmental consequences of impacts, if any, do to
     the location of the facility at the proposed site.
     Both short and long term consequences will be
     considered.

- Mitigation of adverse environmental impacts hopefully to a level of insignificance.
- Mitigation of adverse environmental impacts hopefully to a level of insignificance.
- Conclusions regarding the significance of impacts to assist in the determination of a "Finding of no Significant Impact" (FONZI).
- A narrative report of each item and its impact that will be included in the EIS document.

Adherence to statutory requirements. The team members will abide by the requirements of the respective statues applicable to each area of specialty.
These statutes are:

- Archeological Resources Protection Act
- National Historic Preservation Act
- Aboriginal Religious Freedom Act
- Clean Water Act
- Safe Drinking Water Act
- Fish and Wildlife Coordination Act
- Endangered Species Act
- Clean Air Act

A draft EIS document will be prepared for distribution to the appropriate agencies and the public for review and comment.
Assist in the conduct of public meetings/hearings as deemed necessary by the Land Preserve Bureau.

PROJECT APPROACH

The project approach in conducting of the EIS will be ultimately set by the Bureau of Environmental Affairs. Our intent will be to conduct the necessary meetings with the Bureau of Environmental Affairs Staff ta seek information and feedback regarding the approach.
Following is a generalized approach that we intend to utilize.
Meet with production staff of Cripps Chromium Corporation to receive an orientation regarding such things as:

- The Mining process to be utilized
- Chemicals and materials used in the process
- Number and type of vehicles utilizing the access and haul roads
- Waste by-products, nature and quantities
- Schedule of operations
- Method(s) proposed to be utilized to mitigate environmental impacts such as surface and ground water pollution, air quality noise, etc.
- Type and numbers of equipment utilized in the operation

  −   Economic impacts arising from the hiring of human re-
      sources and equipment purchases in the area
  −   Known health affects from similar operations else-
      where.

   Conduct an initiation meeting with the Bureau of Environ-
mental Affairs Staff to establish guidelines regarding:
  −   Lines of communications
  −   Schedules of submittal and reviews
  −   Special requirements to be incorporated in the EIS
      specific to the site.
  −   List of items that will be considered an environmental
      "Fatal Flaw" from the stand point of the Bureau of
      Environmental Affairs
  −   Public participation elements and schedule

   Review the project for environmental "Fatal Flaws". Early
study and implementing appropriate mitigation measures will
help the EIS process proceed smoothly.
   Finalize the EIS document and prepare a camera ready copy
for printing by the Bureau of Environmental Affairs.
   If anytime during the EIS process it is determined that
impact of the proposed action or any alternative upon the
human environment will be significant, we will withhold the
EIS preparation and seek future direction from Cripps Chromium Corp. and the Bureau of Environmental Affairs.

   Project Team: We propose the following project team composition: Proposed organization chart is attached.

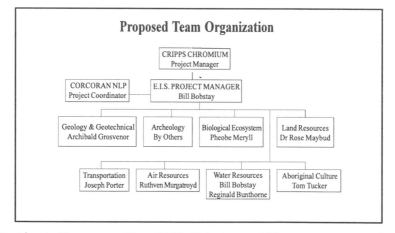

   Project Manager: Mr. Bill Bobstay will serve as project
manager. He will provide the required liaison and coordination with Cripps Chromium staff, various governmental agencies and the public. Mr. Bobstay brings over 2 decades of
professional engineering experience including the conduct
of EA/EIS process and public participation program. Mr.
Bobstay has addressed numerous legislative bodies and pub-

lic meetings and hearings. His confident, comfortable style coupled with cordial attitude toward the audience has been known to streamline the generally controversial nature of EA/EIS public hearings.

As a specialist in Water Resources, Mr. Bobstay will also serve on the team as an active participant in the evaluation of water related impacts. His familiarity with the Safe Drinking Water and Clean Water Acts and his established track record with regulatory agencies will be immensely valuable.

Geology and Geotechnical Impacts Mr. Archibald Grosvenor, a sub-consultant to RTA will serve on the teem and in this capacity will be responsible for evaluating geological and geotechnical impacts. Mr. Grosvenor brings over 10 years of experience in this field all of which has been in Graniola. Mr. Grosvenor has conducted several investigations in Corcoran Township and is intimately familiar with the geology of the area.

Environmental Scientist: Dr. Rose Maybud, a consultant will serve on the project team to assist in the evaluation of land resources, noise and resource use categories. Dr. Maybud brings over 20 years of experience in environmental research in industry, municipal and private projects. In addition to her excellent experience she brings a graduate degree in geology and a doctoral degree in applied earth sciences from Magnate University. The combination of her skills in extractive Metallurgy and environmental issues makes her uniquely qualified for this project.

Ecologist: Ms. Phoebe Meryll will provide specialized evaluations of the vegetation and biological impacts on the ecosystem. Ms. Meryll brings over 15 years of experience in biological and ecological evaluations. Ms. Meryll 's experience in the study of the ecosystem relative to small mammals in the Pisant Mountains and her work connected with EA/EIS for the Land Preserve Bureau is most noteworthy and applicable on this project. Ms. Meryll has served as an independent consultant to the Huh Aboriginal Nation concerning an active nest of Northern Spotted Owl relative to timber sale on the Huh reservation.

Aboriginal Culture and Religion: Mr. Tom Tucker a principal of Rackstraw, Tucker and Associates, Inc. and an Aboriginal by heritage, will serve on the team to provide expertise in this area. Mr. Tucker has provided professional services to numerous Aboriginal reservations for the past 15 years and being an Aboriginal and a native of Graniola brings extensive knowledge of the Aboriginal Culture and Religion.

Transportation: Mr. Joseph Porter, a senior transportation consultant with RTA, will serve on the team to provide the benefit of his decades of experience in transportation system planning, evaluation and design. Mr. Porter has been involved with numerous EIS processes during his 39 years of employment with the Graniola Province Highway and Transportation Department.

Air Resources: Mr. Ruthven Murgatroyd an air quality consultant will be responsible for evaluating air resources for the EIS. Mr. Murgatroyd brings over a decade of air quality experience. His experience is quite unique since he has held responsible positions with regulatory agencies at both the local and province level. He also brings a diversified air quality modeling and permitting experience while serving as a consultant to the industry. His familiarity with the Clean Air Act and first hand knowledge and tract record with the regulatory agencies will be an asset to the team.

Water Resources: Mr. Bill Bobstay will serve on the team relative to water quality impact evaluations. Mr. Reginald Bunthorne, a hydrologist with RTA, will assist in the hydrological assessment of the project. The combined experience of the two team members is over 25 years. Both team numbers bring advanced degrees in Water Resources and Hydrology.

Professional Fees: We are willing to accept a "time and material" or lump sum contract. At this time it is difficult to accurately estimate lump sum fee since exact scope of work is not well defined. The standard hourly billing rates for various staff categories is provided below.

| Project Manager | $70/hr. |
|---|---|
| Geology/Geotechnical Consultant | 65/hr. |
| Biological Ecosystem Scientist | 55/hr. |
| Land Resource Scientist | 60/hr. |
| Transportation Engineer | 60/hr |
| Air Resources | To be retained by Cripps Chromium directly |
| Water Resources Hydrologist | 45/hr. |
| Senior Environmental Engineer | 65/hr. |
| Aboriginal Culture | 55/hr. |

Direct expenses will be billed based on actual out of pocket costs. Mileage reimbursement for automobile will be billed at $.28/mile and for four wheel drive at $.35/mile.

Billing for services will be on a monthly basis commensurate with the progress of work.

Type of Contract: A standard form for authorization of professional services is enclosed for review by Cripps Chromium Corporation. RTA's policy requires that we obtain a bank and two credit references prior to establishing an account.

Schedule: Upon authorization to proceed we are willing to commence work immediately.

## DECIDING WHERE TO START

Perhaps as you read this proposal you felt baffled by the fact that it does not immediately identify the prospective client or the nature of the work proposed. Even in the section called "understanding the scope of work," it's not clear at once that Rackstraw, Tucker is proposing to prepare an environmental impact statement (EIS). So one thing you might want to do is write a new opening section, because you can be sure that proposal evaluators have little patience for mysteries. There goes an hour, by the time you get one of the principals to describe the project a little more clearly and then write it up.

It may have seemed odd to put what looks like boilerplate at the front of the proposal. The sections up to "scope" need to be moved. Typically, in proposals, you try to convince a prospect that you have a well-thought-out strategy for solving the prospect's problem and that you have attached reasonable costs to the doing. Only then is it necessary to show the prospect evidence of previous accomplishments of the company and its staff. If the prospect is not convinced of the cogency of your plan, or if your proposal's arrangement suggests that you wish to be considered more for your reputation than for your having considered the prospect's current needs, your proposal may be pronounced dead on arrival. This one was.

> **Revising to Anticipate Readers' Needs**
> • Orientation: tell readers what they're looking at, and why
> • Access: provide readers the tools to find what they want
> • Smoothness: don't distract readers with glitches and dumb mistakes
> • Comprehension: style the prose for economy and clarity

You probably noticed that the document seems to have no shape—its heart consists mostly of lists, and the headings aren't used with any consistency. The "project approach" section doesn't seem integrated with the list of possible impacts in the previous section. In that list, wildlife, vegetation, and biological ecosystem are parallel, though you might think ecosystem includes the others; earthquakes don't seem much of a land resource. But to fix these problems will require much more than the three hours you have available.

Then there's the prose. What's not in lists seems wooden and sometimes repetitive—"Ms. X brings Y years of experience." You could spend a couple of your precious hours restyling the prose.

And the spelling: someone must have run the document through the spellchecker, but it didn't catch homophone confusions (orifice/office, servile/several, principle/principal, sight/site, etc.) Apparently, the text was originally typed in haste; the spellchecker only made things worse when the keyboarder chose the wrong option among several.

## SNAP DECISIONS

You could use a "Levels of Edit" approach, as discussed at the beginning of the chapter: you could decide, with the proposal manager, to do correctness, policy, integrity, and screening edits. But the "levels" approach needs enough time for the editor to cost out the various options. In this particular case, doing a "levels" assessment will eat up a significant amount of the time available for editing. Another problem is that the proposal manager may choose the lowest–cost option, which is not necessarily the best one. Since your orders are "fix it up," you have to decide what things need fixing most.

You and your company want this proposal to win, but clearly it isn't going to if the people at Cripps can't tell right away what the document is and how RTA proposes to address their concerns. So the first thing you have to do is craft a new front end. How you do this depends on the document format thought to be appropriate: letter proposal from Bobstay to Cripps's contact person, or formal proposal with cover letter? The latter is probably appropriate because a letter proposal shouldn't exceed two pages. A formal proposal also lends itself better to inclusion of access tools.

In the draft, access is a problem. Not only are headings inconsistent, there are some sentence fragments after the "environmental factors" list that might have been intended as headings. Proposal evaluations are often done by teams, with each member taking responsibility for a different aspect. So something must be done to make it easy for evaluators to find things. Straightening out the headings and providing a table of contents takes high priority.

Proposal evaluators are affected by first impressions, so dumb mistakes will detract. A quick scan will probably find most of them.

Allied to dumb mistakes and format/access improvements are some strange spacings as well as inconsistencies in methods of listing. If you have the document on disk, you can use the word processor's style or search-and-replace functions to bring order.

In whatever time is left, you can straighten up tortured syntax. Fortunately for this proposal, there isn't much of it, since so much of the proposal is lists.

Here's the proposal after a three-hour treatment. A few queries need to be settled before the finished copy is run off. Boldface indicates words inserted or moved to new locations; deletions are indicated by lines through words or punctuation. Sections that needed moving have been moved, (In the interests of readability, the movements of sections are not shown by any typographical devices).

**SUMMARY**

Cripps Chromium wishes to open a mining operation in the Corcoran National Land Preserve, Corcoran Township, Graniola. Prior to doing so, it must evaluate this mine's probable impacts on the environment. The necessary environmental impact statement (EIS) and the process leading to it is the subject of this proposal by Rackstraw, Tucker and Associates, Inc.

~~Understanding Of The~~ **SCOPE OF WORK**~~:~~

Based on the meeting of April 22, 1994, the following reflects our understanding of the scope of services.

Cripps Chromium Corporation intends to conduct Chromium Mining operation at the Pinafore Mine within the Corcoran National Land Preserve in Corcoran Township, Graniola. Mining operation is anticipated to commence in 1996.

- Open pit ~~type~~ mining will be utilized. Pit dimensions are anticipated to be 2,000 ft. x 2,000 ft.
- Heap-leach ~~type~~ operation is proposed at this time.
- Approximately 60 million tons of waste material will be generated during the operation. The waste material will include waste rock, tailings, and spent ore.
- Blasting will be utilized.
- Current plans call for creation of a dam on Hebe Creek for stockpiling the ore.
- Major environmental concerns include **the** existence of **a** wilderness boundary near the site.
- Leaching of processing chemicals into natural streams on groundwater [**must be checked**?].
- Impacts related to access and haul roads [**must be evaluated**?].
- All EIS activities must be coordinated with the Corcoran National Land Preserve Staff.
- Work will be p**er**formed in accordance with the memorandum of understanding being executed between Cripps Chromium Corporation and the Bureau of Environmental Affairs, Corcoran National Land Preserve.
- Cripps Chromium Corporation wishes to retain specialty consultants such as archaeologists as independent contractors. RTA will be required to coordinate with these consultants and ~~approximately~~ incorporate ~~the data and~~ **their** information in**to** the EIS.

The project manager will prepare an outline of the EIS document and obtain concurrence from the Bureau of Environmental Affairs. The project manager will **then** assign EIS study tests to the various team members commensurate with their ~~respective~~ areas of expertise.

The EIS will be prepared in accordance with **NEPA** requirements. The elements of the document will include but **will** not necessarily be limited to the following environmental factors.

1. Land Resources~~:~~
   - Topography
   - Soil
   - Geology
   - Drainage and erosion
   - Earthquakes and other natural disasters [**Q: are natural disasters a resource?**]
2. Water Resources~~:~~
   - Surface and ground water quality
   - Use
   - Rights

3. Air Resources~~:~~
   - Quality
   - Permitting **[Q: obtaining of permits?]**
4. Wild Life **[Q: Wildlife?]**
5. Vegetation
6. Biological Ecosystem
7. Agriculture~~:~~
   - Crops
   - Livestock
8. Cultural Resources~~:~~
   - Historic
   - Religious
   - Archaeological
9. Socio-Economic **[Factors?]**~~:~~
   - Employment
   - Attitude
   - Life style
   - Local tax base advantages
10. Resource Use~~:~~
    - Hunting
    - Fishing
    - Crop harvesting
    - Mining
    - Recreation
    - Transportation
    - Other land use
11. Noise
12. Wilderness **[Q: Is this redundant with Resource Use or Vegetation?]**
13. Public Health and Safety

Each team member will evaluate environmental impacts for his/her area of specialty. This evaluation will include the following key elements.

- Collection of historical data and background.
- Environmental consequences of impacts, if any, due to the location of the facility at the proposed site. Both short- and long-term consequences will be considered.
- Mitigation of adverse environmental impacts hopefully to a level of insignificance.

~~Mitigation of adverse environmental impacts hopefully to a level of insignificance.~~

- Conclusions regarding the significance of impacts to assist in the determination of a "Finding of no Significant Impact" (FONZI). **[FONSI?]**
- A narrative report of each item that will be included in the EIS document **and its impact.**

Adherence to statutory requirements. **[Q: is the preceding supposed to be a list item, sentence, or a heading?]**

The team members will abide by the requirements of the
~~respective~~ **following** statutes **as** applicable to each area of
specialty~~.~~:
   ~~These statutes are:~~

- Arch**a**eological Resources Protection Act
- National Historic Preservation Act
- Aboriginal Religious Freedom Act
- Clean Water Act
- Safe Drinking Water Act
- Fish and Wildlife Coordination Act
- Endangered Species Act
- Clean Air Act

A draft EIS document will be prepared for distribution to
the appropriate agencies and the public for review and
comment.
Assist in the conduct of public meetings/hearings as
deemed necessary by the **Bureau of Environmental Affairs.**
**[Q: sentence lacks subject. "RTA staff will assist in . . .?]**

**PROJECT APPROACH**

The project approach in conducting of the EIS will be
ultimately set by the Bureau of Environmental Affairs. Our
intent will be to conduct the necessary meetings with the
Bureau of Environmental Affairs Staff to seek information
and feedback regarding this approach. **We intend to take
this**
   ~~fFollowing is a generalized~~ approach ~~that we intend to~~
~~utilize.~~:

- <u>Meet with production staff of Cripps Chromium Corpora-
   tion</u> to receive an orientation regarding such things
   as:
   - The **Mm**ining process to be utilized
   - Chemicals and materials used in the process
   - Number and type of vehicles utilizing the access and
      haul roads
   - Waste by-products, nature and quantities
   - Schedule of operations
   - Method~~(s)~~ proposed to be utilized to mitigate envi-
      ronmental impacts such as surface and ground water
      pollution, air quality, noise, etc.
   - Type**s** and numbers of equipment utilized in the opera-
      tion
   - Economic impacts arising from hiring human resources
      and **purchasing** equipment in the area
   - Known health **ea**ffects from similar operations else-
      where.
- <u>Conduct an initiation meeting with the Bureau of Envi-
   ronmental Affairs Staff</u> to establish guidelines regard-
   ing:
   - Lines of communications

- Schedules of submittal**s** and reviews
- Special requirements to be incorporated in the EIS specific to the site~~.~~
- List of items that will be considered an environmental "Fatal Flaw" from the standpoint of the Bureau of Environmental Affairs
- Public participation elements and schedule

- <u>Review the project for environmental "Fatal Flaws"</u>. Early study and implementing appropriate mitigation measures will help the EIS process proceed smoothly.
- <u>Finalize the EIS document and prepare a camera-ready copy</u> for printing by the Bureau of Environmental Affairs.

If any time during the EIS process it is determined that impact of the proposed action or any alternative upon the human environment will be significant, we will withhold the EIS preparation and seek future direction from Cripps Chromium Corp. and the Bureau of Environmental Affairs.

**THE FIRM**

Rackstraw, Tucker and Associates, Inc. (RTA) is a small business enterprise incorporated in the Province of Graniola with or~~iff~~ices in Grand Cataract and Cloud City, Graniola. The firm has a staff of 21 engineers, technologist**s**, and support personnel. RTA has provided professional engineering services to ~~servile~~ public and private clients throughout Graniola since 1975.

**Bill Bobstay (P.E. No. 14138), Ralph Rackstraw (P.E. No. 15457), and Tom Tucker (P.E. No. 14424) are the three principals of the firm.** The three principals of RTA together bring over 60 years of professional engineering experience and are Registered Professional **E**ngineers in the Province of Graniola and several other provinces. Mr. Ralph Rackstraw is **also** a registered land surveyor ~~and professional engineer~~ in the province of Graniola. With the addition of Mr. Joseph Porter as a Senior ~~Consultant~~ Transportation **Consultant,** ~~the firm's accumulated~~ total staff experience now ~~accedes~~ **exceeds** 100 years.

The firm utilizes Computer Aided Design (CAD) on most of its projects and is equipped with ~~numerous~~ modern computer hardware and software in addition to state-of-the-art survey instruments.

The firm's clients include the **Graniola Province Highway and Transportation Department,** the City of Grand Cataract, Marigold Township, Corneal Township, City of Cloud City, Becket Community Development Corporation, Horstgraben Land and Development Company, the **Hoh** Nation, and numerous **other** public and private clients throughout Graniola.

RTA carries general and professional liability insurance in units typical for engineering practices in Graniola.

The firm takes pride in aggressive project management and

active involvment of the principals in project design, quality assurance, and construction administration. **Each of the three principals actively participates in the design, quality assurance, construction phase, and project management of the firm's projects.**

Over eighty percent (80%) of the firm's gross revenues come from repeat clients, which speaks well of our reputation.

### 1.2 THE PRINIPALS

~~All of the principals are registered professional engineers in the Province of Graniola. Mr. Rackstraw is also a registered land surveyor in the Province of Graniola.~~

~~The Graniola registration number of the three principals are provided below.~~

~~Bill Bobstay, P.E. Graniola (P. E. No. 14138 )~~
~~Ralph Rackstraw, P.E. , L.S. Graniola (P.E. No. 15457 )~~
~~Tom Tucker, P.E. Graniola (P. E. No. 14424 )~~

### PROJECT TEAM

~~Project Team:~~ We propose the following project team composition: Proposed organization chart is attached.

Project Manager: Mr. Bill Bobstay will ~~serve as~~ be project manager. He will provide the required liaison and coordination with Cripps Chromium staff, various governmental agencies, and the public. Mr. Bobstay brings over **two** decades of professional engineering experience, including the conduct of EA/EIS process and public participation program. Mr. Bobstay has addressed numerous legislative bodies and public meetings and hearings. His confident, comfortable style, coupled with cordial attitude toward the audience, has been known to streamline the generally controversial nature of EA/EIS public hearings.

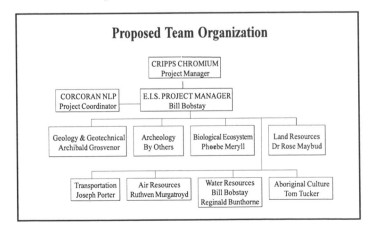

**Proposed Team Organization**

As a specialist in Water Resources, Mr. Bobstay will also serve on the team as an active participant in the evaluation of water related impacts. His familiarity with the Safe Drinking Water and Clean Water Acts and his established track record with regulatory agencies will be immensely valuable.

Geology and Geotechnical Impacts: Mr. Archibald Grosvenor, a sub-consultant to RTA, will serve on the team and in this capacity will be responsible for evaluating geological and geotechnical impacts. Mr. Grosvenor brings over 10 years of experience in this field, all of which has been in Graniola. Mr. Grosvenor has conducted several investigations in Corcoran Township and is intimately familiar with the geology of the area.

Environmental Scientist: Dr. Rose Maybud, a consultant, will serve on the project team to assist in the evaluation of land resources, noise, and resource use categories. Dr. Maybud brings over 20 years of experience in environmental research in industry, municipal and private projects. In addition to her excellent experience she brings a graduate degree in geology and a doctoral degree in applied earth sciences from ~~Magnate~~ **Stanford** University. The combination of her skills in extractive metallurgy and environmental issues makes her uniquely qualified for this project.

Ecologist: Ms. Phoebe Meryll will provide specialized evaluations of the vegetation and biological impacts on the ecosystem. Ms. Meryll brings over 15 years of experience in biological and ecological evaluations. Ms. Meryll 's experience in the study of the ecosystem relative to small mammals in the Pisant Mountains and her work connected with EA/EIS for the **Bureau of Environmental Affairs** is most noteworthy and applicable on this project. Ms. Meryll has served as an independent consultant to the **Hoh Indian** Nation concerning an active nest of Northern Spotted Owl relative to timber sale on the **Hoh** reservation.

Aboriginal Culture and Religion: Mr. Tom Tucker, a principal of Rackstraw, Tucker and Associates, Inc., and an aboriginal by heritage, will serve on the team to provide expertise in this area. Mr. Tucker has provided professional services to numerous aboriginal reservations for the past 15 years and, being an aboriginal and a native of Graniola, brings extensive knowledge of the aboriginal culture and religion.

Transportation: Mr. Joseph Porter, a senior transportation consultant with RTA, will serve on the team to provide the benefit of his decades of experience in transportation system planning, evaluation and design. Mr. Porter has been involved with numerous EIS processes during his 39 years of employment with the Graniola Province Highway and Transportation Department.

Air Resources: Mr. Ruthven Murgatroyd, an air quality consultant, will be responsible for evaluating air resources for the EIS. Mr. Murgatroyd brings over a decade of air quality experience. His experience is ~~quite~~ unique, since he has held responsible positions with regulatory agencies at both the local and province level. He also brings a diversified air quality modeling and permitting experience while serving as a consultant to the industry. His familiarity with the Clean Air Act and first hand knowledge and track record with the regulatory agencies will be an asset to the team.

Water Resources: Mr. Bill Bobstay will serve on the team relative to water quality impact evaluations. Mr. Reginald Bunthorne, a hydrologist with RTA, will assist in the hydrological assessment of the project. The combined experience of the two team members is over 25 years. Both team ~~numbers~~ **members** bring advanced degrees in Water Resources and Hydrology.

**CONTRACTUAL MATTERS**

Professional Fees: We are willing to accept a "time and material" or lump sum contract. At this time it is difficult to accurately estimate the lump sum fee since **the** exact scope of work is not well defined. The standard hourly billing rates for various staff categories is provided below.

| | |
|---|---|
| Project Manager | $70/hr. |
| Geology/Geotechnical Consultant | 65/hr. |
| Biological Ecosystem Scientist | 55/hr. |
| Land Resource Scientist | 60/hr. |
| Transportation Engineer | 60/hr. |
| Air Resources | To be retained by Cripps Chromium directly |
| Water Resources Hydrologist | 45/hr. |
| Senior Environmental Engineer | 65/hr. |
| Aboriginal Culture | 55/hr. |

Direct expenses will be billed based on actual out-of-pocket costs. Mileage reimbursement for automobile will be billed at $.22/mile and for four wheel drive at $.30/mile.

Billing for services will be on a monthly basis, commensurate with the progress of work.

Type of Contract: A standard form for authorization of professional services is enclosed for review by Cripps Chromium Corporation. RTA's policy requires that we obtain a bank reference and two credit references prior to establishing an account.

Schedule: Upon authorization to proceed we are willing to commence work immediately.

The proposal is still a long way from ideal. It still needs a title page and table of contents. But at least it provides the reader with orientation and access and contains fewer distracting mistakes. With more time, the editor could do more with sentence style. Likewise, with more time the engineers could think through the approach more thoroughly.

# CHAPTER 13

**You** may wonder how technical editors, doing all of this heavy editing, manage to get along with the editees. Well, if you can believe the literature of technical editing, this is one of editors' foremost problems.

# Getting Along with Authors

The difficulty is often blamed on the gap between the two cultures. Too many editors do not understand the scientific copy, and the scientists may not trust them, claiming, "They change my meaning."

But the pride-of-authorship clash occurs also among the practitioners of English technology. As some editors know, the toughest people to edit are writers and editors, especially those who are rule-bound. But as authors inevitably learn, everyone needs an editor, even editors.

What we are hoping to convey is that no matter how much an editor slashes, mutilates, warps, or defaces the copy, or beats, bludgeons, or brutalizes the author, the whole operation must be friendly.

## TYPES OF COLLABORATION

Editors have devised many strategies to get along with authors. Unfortunately, the most common one is to avoid confrontation by making as few marks as possible. This clever ploy is often encouraged by the technical people and, surprisingly, also by some textbooks on technical editing.

Technical editors thus too often retreat into being arbiters of abbreviations, capitalization, hyphening, etc. Some become guardians of the official abbreviations of scientific journals.

Such mechanics may be contained in a company style manual. But unfortunately, these manuals may become overstuffed with pedantic rules and pet peeves, eagerly amassed from questionable nontechnical sources. (See Appendix C, "Style Manuals.") So, as the miscellaneous agglomeration solidifies, it can create a confrontational interface with the authors. (By the way, *interface* may be one of the words the style manual outlaws.)

No wonder new editors are instructed to edit gently and smile a lot.

One veteran editor named Walter Spike had almost the opposite approach. He was asked how he dealt with authors.

"I hit 'em in the stomach," he said. He explained that in any new piece of copy, something will jump out at you: a typo, a grammatical error, a wrong usage. Walter would take out his red pencil and mark the spot very deliberately, saying slowly, "Yes, this may take considerable work."

"It softened them up," claimed Walter.

## RIGIDITY VS. FLEXIBILITY

No editor can be against smiling, nor against style manuals. But engineers, like typists, tend to be "consistency" zealots and view language as being immutable, like algebra. They also may want to dictate which "correctness" principles the style manual contains. And the correctness principles of logistics engineering (say) are almost sure to diverge from those of conventional discourse. Therefore, companywide style manuals can be divisive, and (for the editor in charge) self-destructive.

The problem is that style manuals are too rigid. They may call for hyphens with unit modifiers, for instance. Technically, that means "7-ft-by-9-ft-dia. fairing," with a parade of five hyphens. But since engineers as a tribe hate hyphens, such a locution won't have been used in the RFP. Nevertheless, you may have to use five hyphens in the proposal. Why? Because that's "company style," contained in three big blue binders on each editor's bookshelf.

One widely accepted solution is to modify the style on each proposal to fit the RFP of the particular customer, whenever the RFP is consistent enough to allow it. (See Appendix B, "Editing Technical Proposals.")

In addition, editors always need to be sensitive to the needs of the departments. For Public Relations you definitely need to tolerate the strict newspaper "down" style; for the Research Division you may need to use "data are." For most engineering departments you may want to standardize according to the American Standards Association; for more "academic" authors you may choose to use the American Institute of Physics manual. (They are essentially the same, so conflict is minimal.)

Thus, you attain good communication and persevere not through rigidity, but through wide flexibility.

However, it's important always to have a good reason for every editing mark you make.

## REJECTING THE IMAGE OF LANGUAGE POLICE

Never, never do you enter into pitched battle over the style manual. Save your spleen for something important, like preserving technical accuracy or cutting out that pervasive bombast.

Instead of reflecting an image of "language police," editors need to listen a lot, and help authors develop their messages as well as deliver them. One effective technique is to ask questions. If you express interest in a project, the writers become more confident that you won't change their meaning.

## THE TWO CULTURES

One problem that exists today in technical editing is that the editors may have their own room, down the hall, away from the action. They may seldom come within shouting distance of the authors. Perhaps, however, they keep track of blunders, and their opinion of the authors may be very low.

The authors' opinions of the editors is probably still lower. Any conversation between them is quiet and even-tempered, but stress is high and the anguished lyric rings clear: "You changed my meaning." The two groups may never associate or become friendly.

Another problem often widens the chasm. Some young, liberal arts editors disdain technical people, who may not know the difference between James Joyce and Joyce Kilmer. The editors may assume the role of pedagog, laying down rules about grace and grammar that are far away from mil specs.

Or more often, editors may retreat into their corners, devoting their time to policing safe subjects like hyphens and capitals. Here they get fewer gripes, but they also do less good. They become experts on matters that don't mean much to either the authors or the evaluators. Meanwhile, they lose still more face-to-face contact, sacrificing a chance for friendship and for collaborative improvement in both technical clarity and literary quality.

One graduate student in the English Department at the University of New Mexico tells how he once had a job proofreading for a law firm in San Francisco. He became so proficient that he expanded into copyreading and became the resident expert on tense, person, parallelism, and the nonrestrictive phrase. For such pedantic corrections, he said, the lawyers began to view him as a sort of insurance policy for their writing. Once he had given his okay, they felt they could release their documents to the world without fear of ridicule.

Unfortunately, he related, he became a victim of his own success. He was asked to hire more people and start reading everything the firm wrote.

But then editing became automatic, and he lost his personal contact. This was more serious than he thought. The lawyers began to see editing as a routine that occurred just before final type and added to the already considerable delay. Instead of being a valued treatment for individuals, it became an impersonal procedure that happened to the documents. It became part of the problem. A friendly, cooperative arrangement had become adversarial.

Shortly thereafter, he left. The lesson to him was clear. When dealing with authors, keep up your face-to-face contact.

Young editors need to resign themselves to serving clients who smell like chemistry labs. They need to learn what the authors want and help them to achieve it. They need to apply their linguistics training and learn engineering idiom as a second language (EISL). They need to help technical authors say what they want to say in the way the customer wants to hear it.

In short, editors need to "join the team," getting to know each author personally, and perhaps moving onto the project, pencils and all. They will soon find that they enjoy playing bridge with the authors at lunchtime, going to their project parties, and perhaps becoming close personal friends.

## THE TECHNIQUE OF BUSHWHACKING

When editing technical documents, you don't have to pussyfoot. In fact, you may get away with what some engineers have come to call "bushwhacking," cutting through the thickets and removing up to one-third of the underbrush. It won't be long before you will begin to encourage the authors to write their sections a bit long (not that they need that encouragement) so that you can tighten up the wordiness and to get them into their allotted space. This makes engineers happy.

You're smart if not all of your editing marks are negative. Be sure to praise good writing highly. One proposal editor even bought small boxes of gold stars, and occasionally plastered one at the top of a deserving submission. The surprised authors loved it, because on proposals praise was so unexpected.

Editors may never have any power. Their marks may be doomed to be suggestions only; authors can take them or not. (They may actually take only about 90 percent, which is fine.) Editors should not argue unless the author's decision affects technical accuracy. The few barbarisms they leave salt the proposal with engineering flavor and help cover up any taste of public relations slickness.

It's sometimes hard for "stylebook" editors to swallow this; however, the goal of technical editing is not to adhere to a motley high school version of "correctness," but to communicate technical ideas intelligently to the critical and powerful readers, in their own language.

## OTHER TYPES OF EDITING

Heavier editing is probably needed on proposals than on other types of reports. But you can bushwhack almost everything. The main thing you probably should spare is signed articles, where authors really do have the right to be wordy if they choose. And besides, they often need vapid verbiage to fill up space.

On the other hand you can use heavy editing on brochures, newsletters, white papers, project descriptions, memos, and the rest. You can cut most manuals drastically, reducing them to 1-2-3 instructions, thereby saving both company money and operator time. You can reorganize them to make their instructions "user-friendly," which is a different thing from "friendly." A "friendly" manual may have a chatty, even ironic, "voice," which doesn't guarantee that a reader can readily find useful information.

## LET AUTHORS HAVE THEIR WORDS

Perhaps the most important strategy editors should use to get along with authors is to try to project mutual cooperation instead of confrontation. You have to take a page from linguistics study, part of the technology of English, and encourage authors to use their own departmental idiom. Then, magically, you will be seen as being on their side. A maintainability engineer writes differently from an aerodynamicist, and both of them write differently from an expert on artificial intelligence.

As we have said before, the maintainability engineer who is writing to another maintainability engineer should use the jargon of their mutual profession, not a sanitized universal company language.

To quote STC Fellow Ernie Mazzatenta, writing in *Technical Editing* by Carolyn Rude (1991), two things writers dislike about editors are that (1) they replace words with synonyms and (2) they use words that are not acceptable to the writer or others and will not change them.

Editors should not argue about words. They should make the editing changes in the structure, but leave the technical words alone!

Veteran wordsmiths find that authors seldom mind if editors recast their sentences, no matter how drastically. You can easily reverse "The dial must be monitored by the technician" to "The technician must monitor the dial." The author seldom says, "That's better." But he may say, "That's OK. It doesn't make any difference."

Aha! Then both of you can be happy, because editors know that sentence structure does indeed make a marvelous difference in communication. You can put the verb next to the subject and put the most powerful word at the end, and even cut out the deadwood without raising any hackles.

But if you ever change the Latin "in situ" to the English "in place" you will be almost sure to hear the wail, "You changed my meaning." And indeed, you may have impeded communication. The two locutions, say the experts, don't mean the same thing.

Scientists get to be set in their ways. They actually seem to like the rhythm of words like *utilize* and *approximately*. Therefore editors know that when they use synonyms, they're risking a fight, no matter how much they smile.

## SUGGESTIONS ON IMPROVING RELATIONS

Editors can do a number of things to improve relations with authors. Some of them are radical but may be worth considering in an effective editing program. Hang on.

Editors are taught to eschew Latin, but instead, what if we welcomed it? Experts say that most obfuscation comes not from vocabulary but from structure. Phrases like "in situ" cause no confusion to the technical audience and show that the author is a knowledgeable part of the technical team. After all, the object is to help writers communicate in the language of the reader.

What about grammar? Too often new editors change "a design criteria" to "a design criterion," not realizing that structures engineers don't always discourse in the language of H. W. Fowler. Moreover, rules of grammar, when applied too strictly, tend to make our language "sound funny." "It is I?" "And then there was none?" Most veteran editors and college English teachers are united on this point. (See Chapter 8, "Grammar.")

And how about jargon? As we have mentioned, editors are taught that scientific reports are "formal" and must be impeccably dignified. But jargon is how engineers talk to each other, and an occasional lapse into these words, and even slang, will not destroy a scientific report, but instead will add life and vitality.

Now comes the controversial part. What if editors relaxed a bit in enforcing that style manual? Most style prohibitions deal not with structure, but with individual words. Is it any wonder that editors and authors have a thorny interface? Of what value is "consistency" if it (1) arouses conflicts and (2) actually hinders natural, idiomatic communication between authors and their technical audience?

## CONCLUSION

We can never eliminate style manuals, grammar books, dictionaries, and other standards. But we can soften the rigid approach, which often comes across as stubbornness. We editors need to reject the image of language police and join the team.

In short, the goal in editing is not to resist every minor incursion against "correctness"; it is to facilitate communication.

After all, technical people don't send many proposals to English teachers. One editor tells about finding in a request for proposal five grammatical errors in the first five sentences. He said to himself, "What am I doing here?"

What he was doing there was improving communication. Often, instead of "correcting" *data is*, editors help more by slashing and thrashing the weedy underbrush, leaving entirely new sentences that are clear, precise, idiomatic, and basically correct. In most engineering writing it's not hard to improve clarity and precision.

Technical people know that they need help. If they get the editor's okay, they can release their documents to the world without fear of ridicule. And maybe they can win a proposal, or even write a paper that is widely read! But this will never happen if the relationship becomes adversarial.

On the other hand, as many veteran editors can testify, a friendly liberal arts major can become a welcome addition to a rigidly trained, but warm and fuzzy, bunch of technical people.

---

**ADVICE IN DEALING WITH AUTHORS**

1. Join the team. You are not grading papers, you are trying to get a message across. Don't consider editing a battle. Try to find out what the author wants to say and help her say it. Ask questions.

2. Let the small things go. Save your righteous indignation for important details, like technical accuracy. (Only you and the reader may know when bad syntax distorts *technical* meaning.)

3. Challenge facts first, wording second. Check numbers. Check the basic outline, the organization, the logic, sequences. Check what's left out.

4. Use the natural, standard idiom of the language.

5. Learn to cut copy without losing information. Authors appreciate your help, particularly on proposals, manuals, memos, and bulletins.

6. Edit heavily on proposals and manuals, but take it easy on signed articles.

7. Have good reasons for everything you do.

8. Learn to reward good writing with a note at the top. Recognition will breed more good work.

9. Smile. Be pleasant, agreeable, accommodating, and helpful.

# APPENDIX

Most people hired as "technical writers" work on technical manuals.

The technical writing profession itself burgeoned during and after World War II because of the need for military handbooks. Then, just as it seemed to be on the verge of a decline, along came the computer; with the computer came software, and with software the need for user manuals.

At this writing, most user manuals are long, wordy, disorganized, and repetitious. For editors, this is a potential opportunity. It won't be long before industry realizes that it can chop down that volume of copy, thereby saving time and cost and also improving user access; it's a win-win situation. Good editing can help communication immensely by spotting irrelevancies, eliminating repetition, and condensing language drastically, reducing inconvenience as well as the costs of paper, warehousing, and drayage.

Editing may be especially important in software manuals, because jumbled instructions may cause users to suspect that they are not getting logical, efficient programming in the product itself.

Today most firms that produce software manuals do indeed have teams of editors. But these editors, though conscientious, are reluctant to cut and rearrange the programmers' copy, preferring to focus on the "consistency" of capitalization, abbreviations, etc. It follows that since consistency can largely be checked by computer, these editors may have only the status of typists, often even sitting in with them and reporting to the head keyboarder (who nowadays, as Production Manager, may boss all editing decisions).

So it is no wonder that editors are underpaid, while the language in manuals is less than perfect. The situation is not helped, either, by national competitions that seem to value artwork, design, and the overweening "consistency" over the important topics of organization, economy of words, and, most important, manual accessibility.

# Editing Technical Manuals

## DEFINING AND DESCRIBING

Actually, as we have said, the ultimate mission of the technical editor is not just to fix mistakes, but to promote communication.

In a user manual, for example, as suggested by Edmond Weiss in *How To Write Usable User Documentation* (1991), instead of giving the operator elaborate instructions on how to use software, editors can someday help design the software itself, making it more understandable, more communicative. Editors can bring to this problem their special skills in communication and cognition. As more and more instruction goes "on line," the editor's role will evolve more and more toward design participation.

In other words, instead of writing about how to obey warning labels, they should concentrate on rewriting the labels themselves, to make them clear. Or they can even point out defects in human–machine interfaces such as keyboards. On some machines, the CAPS LOCK key is far too handy; clumsy keyboarders wish they had been in on the ground floor in that design.

But technical editors can attack problems that are even more significant than that. Technical documenters are the first users of any software system. As they learn more and more about the system, they can begin to validate the software as they go along, getting help in changing sequences that are awkward or difficult.

Weiss says, "Technical writers can discover ways to improve the system that developers are unable to see. Documenters who discover flaws soon enough can eliminate many pages of tortuous documentation."

He suggests that a good goal would be to make software so simple that no manual is required. He asks, "Why are we still laboring to document systems that with the right menus and help screens would need little paper documentation?"

This is the new wave, and, paradoxically, working to eliminate manuals is a good way for smart manual editors to preserve their jobs. However, they must be smart and be willing to work with the technical people to learn the internal workings of the products.

If you've ever tried to use the on-line help that comes with your personal computer software, you've surely experienced readerly frustration. Much on-line help seems friendly enough, even being organized around the question "How do I . . . ?" But the screen never answers the more important question "Why would I . . . ?" And when the user does have a "how do I" question, it's commonly not listed. Perhaps the documentation writers don't run into the same problems. Perhaps they focus their writing on the program's features more than on the readers' needs.

## CONTENT

Technically, there are three kinds of manuals: a tutorial, a reference, and a combination.

Tutorial manuals offer training keystroke by keystroke. They are hard to write well. Top brass may reject them intuitively without actually knowing what's wrong (a familiar writer's lament). All they know is that the opus lacks tutorial material; it does not "tutor." This is a deficiency that editors should be prepared to remedy.

A good tutorial proceeds step by step, with frequent examples, providing any background too elaborate for the screen to accommodate. This process takes time and space, but it's impressive to the brass, and to users.

The need for tutorials is often overstated. User requirements vary widely, but most users, even beginners, don't need them. So perhaps the most useful manuals after all are short, handy, memory-jogging references, or checklists.

Some authors call their manuals "combinations," perhaps because they combine the skeleton information of a reference with the bulky package of a tutorial. In some massive volumes the only actual instructions may be INSTALL, LOAD, RUN, and SAVE. Then the user can only hope that the software, when installed, has adequate menus and "Help" cues on screen.

## HOW TO EDIT MANUALS

As an editor of manuals, you will want to follow these basic laws:

- Use short words, short sentences, and a simple style. Cut the deadwood; get to the point. (See Chapter 3, "Copy Cutting.")
- Fundamentally, follow step-by-step chronological order.
- Group related things together; don't skip around. Combine similar thoughts, for conciseness.
- Use the imperative-mood, verb-first sentences. ("Tote that barge.") But put the orientation first and the action last. "Press F9 to exit" becomes "To exit, press F9."
- In most cases, prefer lists to paragraphs.
- Worry less than usual about "sentence variety" or even about word repetition.
- Make sure the copy is clean of spelling and grammatical errors and typos. (Your software can help with this.)

There is good editing advice in the literature. Jonathan Price in *How to Write a Computer Manual* (1984) talks about "the dead hand" that mummifies "I decided" into "it was decisionized."

"Turn clunky nouns (modulation, utilization) back into verbs (modulate, use)," Price says. He also advocates using *I* and *we* and the active voice.

Edmond Weiss cogently says that writers and editors can be helped by considering documents not as works of art, but as devices.

"Writers who think of themselves as artists," he says, "spend most of their time writing and polishing the draft." In contrast, if a document is a device, then the creativity is in engineering what that draft is going to say.

## IMPROVING MANUALS

Most users agree that technical manuals need improvement. Weiss says, "Many of the manuals written—even by the most sophisticated firms—are ineffective: clumsy, inaccessible, and inaccurate.

"How is it," he asks, "that companies are smart enough to design an automated teller or a CAD/CAM system, but cannot manage to write an intelligible user manual?"

Manuals most of all lack accessibility. Thus, they obviously need at least three things to help the reader:

- A table of contents
- An index
- Clear headings

However, even poor manual writers are well aware of these three requirements and may treat them as a panacea. They often supply oversized headings, shouting at the reader two or three times per page. They may supply multiple tables of contents: a long version and a short version. One recent Navy manual of 200 pages had seven tables of contents: one for each of six sections and one up front to tell the reader which of the six sub-tables to use.

But the reader yearns to be able to find easily the answers to simple questions, like "How can I draw pictures?" She may not be able to find answers because of all the clutter. Large headings and multiple tables of contents simply magnify her problem, and "pictures" isn't listed in the index.

More is not always better. In fact, accessibility is helped most by two things:

- Structure
- Reduction in the manual's sheer size, through crispness

## THE NEED FOR STRUCTURE

In good manuals, as in good software, you will find a structured, top-down organization: the general to the specific, the main categories to the details, the simple to the complex. Unfortunately, though, even after all these years of touting "top-down," the software industry still produces some manuals "topsy-turvy."

Here are a few tips for editors on achieving structure:

- First decompose the material into coherent parts.
- Then subdivide and resubdivide each part so that each process has no more than six or seven short steps. (Be sure to separate steps from results.)
- Number each step so you can refer back to it.
- Explain the big picture in a brief summary at the start.

The summary at the front can be written last. It need not be long; sometimes one good sentence will do. But it should discuss the subject, and not the manual. Especially avoid an extra table of contents that intones "Chapter 1 contains . . . , Chapter 2 contains . . ." and which leaves no clue about the software.

Just note the professional manuals that accompany your appliances at home; they probably (1) start with the name and model of the appliance and (2) summarize what it is equipped to do.

Therefore, an editor can almost automatically eliminate any sentence that begins "This manual . . ." and begin with the first sentence that says "This software. . . ."

Manuals need to introduce the subject. The summary can be used to explain such things as whether users are going to need a hard disk or need to start several days ahead of time, or if the equipment should not be handled by children. In some types of manuals it's often a good idea to list the equipment and supplies that users will need, the way recipes list ingredients. If the author is giving instructions for a step-by-step task, like waxing a table, the editor should make sure that the manual tells first what the user will need.

A summary may divide the task into major parts, like Preparation, Application, and Clean-up. Then the manual itself can proceed to walk the user through the instruction in an orderly hierarchy, class by class, branch by branch, all of it clearly labeled, and also indexed for easy retrieval. (See Chapter 4, on organization.)

Some manuals take the lazy way. Instead of decomposing the problem into sets of smaller things and establishing a logical hierarchy, they treat subjects alphabetically. This puts form lists ahead of menus, pop-up screen elements ahead of screen elements, and windows at the end. Multi-chaos.

Such an "encyclopedia," with separate articles on each subject, seems to some engineers to be the unimpeachable way to organize. But it wastes a lot of space trying to relate *horizontal format,* near the front, with *vertical format,* near the end, requiring either multiple cross references or repetition or both. Besides, it is often difficult for the user to determine whether she will find *horizontal format* under the h's, under the f's, in a separate category like *screen arrangements* or *presentation patterns,* or in *miscellaneous, general.* Even more frequently, important details fall between cracks in the alphabet and are left out entirely. Too often, this alphabetic arrangement, very much *unlike* an encyclopedia, may not provide room to discuss topics in much depth, and is confined to definitions and superficial explanations.

Some manuals do have a good summary, but at the end of the book. That's better than nothing, but in the wrong place.

## WARNINGS AND CAUTIONS

Most steps in a manual follow chronological order, but there is one important exception.

Many processes have steps that are dangerous to people or equipment. And Murphy's Law is always operating: "If anything can go wrong, it will." Therefore, manual writers have learned to make cautions in big letters, even in red letters, to try to prevent The Law from causing too much damage.

One vital thing: warnings need to be placed ahead of the hazardous action; afterwards is too late. For instance, if Step 3 is "Open a can of varnish," the caution "KEEP CONTENTS AWAY FROM OPEN FLAME" must appear well ahead of Step 3. The warning may be out of chronological order, but the practice makes good sense.

## THE NEED FOR CRISPNESS

A good manual will have a smooth, crisp style, written to satisfy the needs of the user. Unfortunately, the emphasis in manuals today is less on crispness and more on chattiness. Certainly, friendliness is important, as discussed below. But the first requirement is something quite different, which is "user-friendliness," or clarity.

As we have said before, manual writing is sometimes gross, not because of the number of gross words, but rather because of the gross number of words. (See Chapter 3, "Cutting Copy.")

Most important, trimming words can promote reader understanding. Many editors own the Strunk-White *Elements of Style*. "Vigorous writing is concise," it says in four words, vigorously.

Here are examples of gross wordiness, taken from actual manuals:

```
You are prompted to enter Y if you want to continue.
```

**If you want to continue, type Y.**

```
The different status statements that may appear are de-
scribed as follows.
```

```
The SYSTEM OUTPUT field specifies where the reports are to
be printed out, either locally or remotely. A local printer
is one attached to the CCU, or to the System Control Unit
(SCU), if one is used. A remote printer, if used, is at-
tached to a W60 or IBM PC terminal. The setting is changed
by pressing on the space bar to toggle between LOCAL PRINTER
and REMOTE PRINTER. Leave the default setting of LOCAL
PRINTER for setup purposes by pressing Enter to accept it.
```

**The SYSTEM OUTPUT field ordinarily displays LOCAL PRINTER,
specifying that the printer is attached to the CCU or a
System Control Unit (SCU). If it is attached to a W60 or an
IBM PC, use the space bar to toggle to REMOTE PRINTER.**

```
On some topologies with average to heavy traffic on the
network, it is natural for applications that transmit data
over the network to have their packets collide with other
data that is being transmitted at the same time.
```

**On networks with heavy traffic, packets may collide with
other data.**

## REPETITION

One rampant form of wordiness is repetition. Sometimes new sections present the same old things, a sign that at least two writers on the project don't speak to each other.

Repetition is indeed useful when:

- It is acknowledged and is purposefully used for emphasis
- It prevents the user from needing to refer to *another* other page

But repetition may get so prevalent that it repeats the picture captions in the text, which is wasteful and often confusing.

The need for a summary at the end of each section is doubtful. It is put there for "recall," but it often has a pedantic quality, vaguely insulting to the intelligent user. The same object can be achieved with a well-organized text and prominent headings. And the cost and bulk are less.

In short, instead of providing recall, the editor of a manual should work on the much more difficult task of providing accessibility.

## WHAT MAKES A GOOD MANUAL?

In summary, what makes a good manual? Here are a few suggestions.

In good manuals you find detail, logically arranged and complete down to the tiniest capillary, with every exception explained concisely and labelled so readers can find it. Such a manual gives the user respect for the depth of the company's research and the skill of its manual writers.

A good manual also has intelligent instruction that does not talk down to the user. "Good detail" doesn't include a diatribe on how to use the DELETE key; space is valuable, and so is the user's pride. A good manual only specifies bare actions, like: "Select the shared publication and press DEL, then click YES to confirm the deletion." This is intelligent instruction.

In good manuals you find freedom from jargon. Even though a manual may define such terms rigidly, definitions are overrated. It's better to use words that don't need defining.

Good manuals have headings, but not too large and not too frequently. They also use running heads at the top of each page. Bad manuals flaunt salesy slogans like YOU WANT IT? YOU GOT IT or OVER 100 YEARS OF EXPERIENCE (which may be the sum of deceptive addition).

Good manuals have sentences that are short and are either periodic, with the punch at the end, or right-branching, with lists left to the end. Such writing is clearer, especially in manuals. (See Chapter 6, "Sentences with Style.")

Good manuals use rigid parallelism. Similarly, good manuals watch out for dangling elements, like "In order to function properly, you must install XYZ software at each workstation."

Good manuals are not afraid to use pronouns. Pronouns are endemic to a smooth, natural style, but manual writers have been unduly warned against them and may write, "The unit can receive messages only if the unit has a clear view."

It goes without saying that manuals should avoid technical errors. This means that the manual writer must know as much as possible about the software. "Learn the lingo fast," says Price. "As soon as anyone on the team drops a new term, ask what it means."

Price concentrates much of his book on making manuals friendly, certainly a concern of editors. "Don't beat up on your reader," he cautions. He warns against "bombarding people with techno-babble" and instead asks writers, alphabetically, to make their manuals "accurate, bright, clean-cut, encouraging, friendly, full of information, kind, quick to help, trustworthy, and well organized."

"Keep it light," he says airily.

## BOOK DESIGN

The design of the book itself needs to be neat, attractive, and again, accessible, following these general guidelines:

- Use plenty of titles and headings.
- Use plenty of artwork, but make it functional, perhaps with computer drawings of computer screens and clear black-and-white photos.
- Avoid expensive internal color, arty design, and fragile die cuts. Instead, spend your money on quality white or near-white paper. Splurge on white space.
- Use serif type (it's more readable), preferably in 10 point. Some manuals must be used by old eyes in less-than-ideal lighting.
- Make bindings colorful for easy identification. Also make them usable and durable. Consider a loose-leaf design. Labeled dividers are also often practical.

## EDITING ON-SCREEN DIRECTIONS

It goes without saying that if crispness is a virtue in hardcopy manuals, it is an absolute necessity in on-screen directions.

Editors must help writers to:

- Reduce the number of instructions
- Reduce their length
- Shorten sentences
- Use graphic, short words
- Use verbs, eliminate adjectives
- Eliminate or combine steps
- Divide compound steps
- Eliminate "background"

There is a danger here. Instructions must still be clear to the user. It's easy for editors to understand the copy they have just butchered; it may not be as easy for the future user. Be particularly wary of "headline English." Do not drop the *the*'s and *a*'s to save space. Phrases like *switch blades* can be ambiguous.

The good news is that editors (and writers), by learning to write on-line copy, can often apply the same principles of crispness to their hard copy writing. Moreover, editing on-line copy is a step in eventually learning how to edit the software itself.

## THE EDITOR'S FUNCTION IN USABILITY TESTING

Technical writing as a profession grew out of the need for military manuals during and after World War II. (This is despite the claim that the first technical writer was Chaucer, because of his famous description of the astrolabe.)

The military is strong on testing for manuals. It ordinarily requires a contractor to run "validation tests" to be sure users can follow the instructions and then conducts "verification" tests on its own.

Unfortunately, testing can become a panacea, taking the place of good design and logical editorial judgment. If a bad manual passes the verification test, it's in; otherwise, it's sent back repeatedly for wasteful trial-and-error rewrites.

Tests are truly needed, of course, and enthusiasm for them is infiltrating the software manual industry.

Judith Tarutz, in *Technical Editing* (1992), tells about "formal tests conducted by human factors engineers in special laboratories equipped with one-way mirrors (and) videocameras and other instruments that record a session of users working with products and using documentation. . . . A software program might record every character a user types. This data can indicate what types of errors users are most likely to make and can lead to improving a product's design. Other testing can show how often or when a user reaches for the manual, how long it takes to find information, and whether it helps the user perform. . . ."

All of this is very expensive, however, so "testing" may essentially fall to the editor. She is the first reader, the first user. As she struggles to understand how to work the system, she becomes a valuable surrogate for the ultimate operator. In addition, of course, she must check to be sure that the instructions and aids are accurate and free of typos, and that the index, table of contents, tabs, running heads, and page numbers are correct. "An editor's work cannot always be spellbinding," says Tarutz.

Jonathan Price, in *How to Write a Computer Manual* (1984), has a long list of questions an author should ask herself during usability tests. Many of these can be partially (but not ever completely) anticipated by an experienced editor:

- Do the explanations make sense?
- Are they in the right spot?
- Do people know why they should do each step?
- Which passages are murky—and why?

- Are you talking above their heads or beneath their contempt?
- Do you carry on too long about some things?
- Does everything you say hold true on all possible systems with all possible hardware hooked up?
- Can people find things in the index, table of contents, and quick-reference chart?

There are many traps in usability testing that are related to the editorial function. For many readers, the big problem is access, or finding the right instructions to read.

Usability tests are generally conducted on individual sections and therefore do not detect this problem.

Moreover, access is difficult to fix. Once a manual is "completed," authors are reluctant to tear up the organization to remedy a deficiency in planning. Therefore, as related by Ed Weiss in *How to Write Usable User Documentation*, they "patch and plug until the problem appears to go away." Updates pose a similar problem.

Weiss also points out that material that serves well in a usability test is often clumsy for the more experienced reader. (The problem is even more acute on-line.)

All of this points to the benefits of using experienced editors in the first place. Good editors can help the team avoid some of the many pitfalls and keep tests on schedule and within budget.

## THE FUTURE OF MANUALS

Weiss points out the growing need for the manual writer to know the system he is trying to describe. We are entering an era, he says, in which the people who used to write manuals are often engaged instead in redefining systems that won't need so much instruction.

"Why," he asks, "are we still laboring to document systems that, with better user interface (menus and "Help" screens), would need little paper documentation?"

Paradoxically, reducing the amount of documentation may increase the opportunities for good editors. This is because it will separate the editors who understand the manuals' content from those who merely labor to achieve consistency. Technical editors who understand the system will be able to edit the software itself, simplifying and condensing procedures and showing the programmer how to design simpler methods. Then the few instructions that are needed can go on line.

Thus, in the future, even as the number and size of hard copy manuals declines, knowledgeable people predict that there will be a continuing increase in the need for good technical editing.

## CRITERIA FOR AN INSTRUCTIONAL MANUAL

- If it is a reference manual (checklist), is it easy to reference? Is it short? Clear?
- If a tutorial, does it go step by step, explaining each screen, each keystroke?
- If a combo, does it meet both of these requirements?
- Does it start with a summary of the *software* (or hardware) rather than a summary of the *manual* (except in a Preface)?
- Look at the Table of Contents. Is the manual organized top-down according to some logical pattern, or is it just thrown together chronologically or alphabetically?
- Does the manual seem orderly, or confusing?
- Does it contain what seems to be good, precise detail?
- Is the jargon easy to follow, even to an outsider?
- Are the instructions grammatically parallel?
- Is the writing style smooth, crisp? Is it too wordy? Does it repeat itself frequently?
- Could it be shorter?
- Is the tone friendly, or is it indifferent? Does it have a light touch, or a dead, impersonal hand? On the other hand, is it really user-friendly or just chatty?
- Does the author seem to write down to the "stupid operator"?
- Is the writing too salesy?
- Does the manual use short sentences? Periodic sentences?
- Do you find any mistakes in grammar? Spelling? Consistency?
- Do you spot any technical errors? Any other "gotchas"?
- Does the book have good headings? Does it have running heads?
- Does it have good, instructive graphics?
- Is the print readable? Illustrations clear?
- Does the manual have an index?
- Is the book attractive? Are cover, binding, paper durable?
- Does it look too expensive?
- Are there any other pluses or minuses?

# APPENDIX

## Editing Technical Proposals

Paradoxically, in today's world brilliant technical experts are often forced to seek new business by pursuing a skill at which they may be notably inept: writing. In short, they have to put their worst foot forward and submit proposals for new business.

This leaves a great opportunity for technical editors. Editors are experts in writing and document design, and, if given a chance, can magically massage the crudely wrought copy into convincing prose.

And today, editing magic is needed more than ever. Unfortunately, the craft of writing proposals has veered away from thoughtful exposition into the world of hype. Beginning back in the 1960s, proposal writing has more and more become a separate, distinct process of its own, embracing elaborate "prewriting," with themes, walls, mockups, and red teams. It is all done in the name of "planning," but in reality it is bureaucratic chaos. If a typical modern proposal team ever undertook to write *Aviation Week,* it would come out *Aviation Quarterly.*

Here, in the maelstrom of activity, the talents of editors may be submerged, as they have to staff the many gofer jobs: logging art, running copies, enforcing schedules, and taping and retaping successions of drafts along the walls of the proposal room.

Companies have come to impose these convulsions for the sake of "efficiency," but the documents themselves still continue to be dull, cluttered, imprecise, and self-deluding. According to one source, 75 percent are even unresponsive.

"Next time," losing proposal teams vow, "we'll write louder."

## THE MARKETEERS

How did these strange, convoluted, over-eager, time-gobbling rites ever originate? From writers? From professional publishers? From editors? Certainly not.

Unfortunately, proposal management has been usurped by nomadic bands of smooth-talking proposal marketeers. Undeniably, these visiting experts are amiable people and hard workers, and they often have good ideas. But they are seldom skilled authors and they tend to subordinate writing quality to seduction of the customer. Thus, the end product is frequently a braggadocio SELL, SELL, SELL, dominated by blustering boasts about past glories. Editors know that this is hardly artful seduction.

Meanwhile, management knows deep-down that the prewriting ritual doesn't really work, so they bring in "red teams" to make authors engage in a frantic scramble to rewrite at the last minute the perfectly planned document.

## THE HIERARCHY OF HYPE

It is never enough for a writer to be clear, logical, and "salesy." Unfortunately, the proposal may end up being also trite and sophomoric. It may even bore the bidder and run the risk of insulting the customer, all because of the overweening hierarchy of hype.

The hierarchy works like this. The marketeers talk down to the writers, using a child-like language of *war rooms*, *ghosts*, and *tiger teams*. But, more worrisome, they also encourage the writers to talk down to the customer by using headlines, arrows, cartoons, and flagrant over-explanations. "WRITE CLEARLY and REPEAT OFTEN," they shout, implying that the customer is really dumb.

Unfortunately, however, this simplistic approach may backfire, and instead cause the not-so-dumb customer to reflect on the intelligence of the proposal writers.

Editors indeed need to strive for proposals that are clear. But these proposals must also have something exciting to say. They must be crammed full of ideas, not turgid repetition, and must be addressed to people we like and respect, not people who are "really dumb." The customer does not want a gush of glittering generalities about the corporate successes of yesterday; he wants good technical ideas for tomorrow.

To say it another way, an intelligent proposal reflects enthusiasm for the work, not the contract.

## WHAT'S WRONG WITH "KNOW-HOW"

Companies love to talk about themselves. The marketeers know this, and frequently recommend as a theme "Experience." This gambit allows the company to naively *talk* about its expertise instead of *showing* it by tackling the technical problems. The engineering proposal example in Chapter 12 shows this tendency. Perhaps the most over-used word in the lexicon of proposals is "know-how."

It's sometimes a hard idea for an editor to sell to management, but a proposal should focus not on your company, but on the customer. Emphasize your features, and what's unique about them, but promote the features the customer wants.

Match your product to the customer's requirements. This does not mean you just list customer requirements and check them off. That's dull, and may not present most of your company's advantages, which may not be on the customer's list.

## HOW TO SAVE DAYS

No proposal goes perfectly; in fact, our nation's most talented high-tech staffs are daily developing inventive new ways to screw them up.

Companies generally develop a hierarchy of planning charts to help team leaders with scheduling work on proposals. This chart (Figure B.1), used with felt-tip markers to draw horizontal lines, becomes a rudimentary schedule chart (refer to Figure 10.4). The chart showed the proposal process, and it made sure that time was allowed for editing. The problem for editors is that schedules inevitably slip.

Proposals need *extensive* planning. You need to start as much as a year or more ahead to refine your product, figure out what the RFP will say, determine the "discriminators" between you and your competitors, and make a strategic plan.

But a company shouldn't wear out the team with a preliminary pink-paper practice proposal. These proposals are hard work, and by the time the RFP arrives people will have lost not only their psyched-up "Will to Win" enthusiasm, but even their physical energy.

And teams should cut down on the prewriting. The minute the RFP arrives, someone smart should write a master proposal outline *overnight*, with assignments and page allocations. Remember, the entire high-paid team is waiting, and the task is not that tough; you copy the RFP. Exactly.

## STORYBOARDS

For section outlines, the project team may decide to use *storyboards*. These are two-page modules first devised in the 1960s. On the left page is a "theme" and an outline of the proposed text; on the right page is a sketch of the proposed art. (See Figure B.2.)

One advantage of storyboards is to give authors approved outlines. A major disadvantage, though, is that they usurp precious time. The bombastic storyboard "themes" may be reviewed over and over in hot, overpopulated, late-night, dog-and-pony shows that are overgrown versions of the notorious Hollywood story conferences. Participants may claim to be working on the "big picture," but in reality they spend weeks squabbling about tiny details of layout. Unfortunately, this process is especially popular with people who would rather talk than write.

Typically, the project ultimately finds itself with a bombastic outline and not enough days left to get anything on paper except a bragging, superficial proposal.

## Proposal Schedule

Project Title _____ Client _____

RFP No. _____ Submission Date/Time _____ / _____
<br>mo  day  yr  hr  AM/PM

Proposal Class *   1 p   2 p   3 p   Proposal Team _____
<br>in charge

Expected Length: _____ pp. + _____ pp. = _____ pp.
<br>(2# Rough Draft   Original   Boilerplate   Total

| Step   Date Elapsed Day | 1 | 2 | 3 | 4 | 5 | 6 | 7 | 8 | 9 |
|---|---|---|---|---|---|---|---|---|---|
| 1. Lead Assignment _____ | | | | | | | | | |
| 2. Identify & Recruit Key Team Members _____ | | | | | | | | | |
| 3. Strategy Session | | | | | | | | | |
| a. Outline Work Approach _____ | | | | | | | | | |
| b. Outline Proposal & Establish Format _____ | | | | | | | | | |
| c. Establish Proposal Schedule & Budget _____ | | | | | | | | | |
| d. Assign Staff Responsibilities for Proposal _____ | | | | | | | | | |
| 4. Supervisor Approval of Work Plan _____ | | | | | | | | | |
| 5. Technical Proposal Draft Preparation _____ | | | | | | | | | |
| a. Original Material | | | | | | | | | |
| (1) Work Program _____ | | | | | | | | | |
| (2) Project Organization, Management & Scheduling _____ | | | | | | | | | |
| (3) Background, Scope, Approach, etc. _____ | | | | | | | | | |
| b. Boilerplate | | | | | | | | | |
| (1) Company Description _____ | | | | | | | | | |
| (2) Quals _____ | | | | | | | | | |
| (3) Bios _____ | | | | | | | | | |
| 6. Develop Case Management Plan _____ | | | | | | | | | |
| 7. Team Rview of Steps 5a and 6 _____ | | | | | | | | | |
| 8. Pricing (with Contracting Office) _____ | | | | | | | | | |
| 9. Edit Draft | | | | | | | | | |
| a. Original Material _____ | | | | | | | | | |
| b. Boilerplate _____ | | | | | | | | | |
| 10. Team Review of Proposal Draft _____ | | | | | | | | | |
| 11. Supervisor Review & Approval _____ | | | | | | | | | |
| 12. Divisional Review & Approval _____ | | | | | | | | | |
| 13. Corporate Review & Approval _____ | | | | | | | | | |
| 14. Final Revisions of Draft Proposal _____ | | | | | | | | | |
| 15. Contracting Sign-off _____ | | | | | | | | | |
| 16. Final Typing & Proc | | | | | | | | | |
| a. Original Material _____ | | | | | | | | | |
| b. Boilerplate _____ | | | | | | | | | |
| c. Cost Proposal _____ | | | | | | | | | |
| 17. Artwork _____ | | | | | | | | | |
| 18. Order Covers _____ | | | | | | | | | |
| 19. Final Check _____ | | | | | | | | | |
| 20. Printing & Binding _____ | | | | | | | | | |
| 21. Delivery _____ | | | | | | | | | |

NOTES:
<br>*Proposal Classes–       1. Project over $500,000 (follow all steps described above)
<br>2. Project from  $100,000–$500,000 (delete Step 13)
<br>3. Project under $100,000 (delete Steps 12 and 13)

## FIGURE B.1

Storyboard

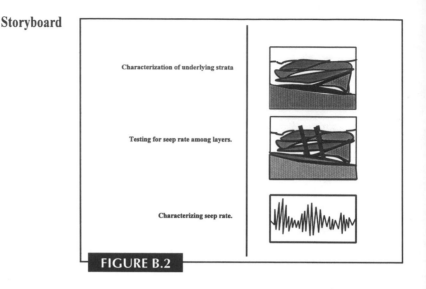

**FIGURE B.2**

## MANAGING STORYBOARDS

Companies frequently discover the hard way that storyboards are no panacea. But the next time, instead of simplifying the process, they grimly impose functions that are even more elaborate, like, say, "proposal document worksheets" or "prereview reviews."

The way to save days is to go the other way. Reject the idea of more bureaucracy and adopt a modern system with only one storyboard requirement: 50 percent artwork.

Storyboards are just outlines; editors should not spend time refining their language! Actually, they should probably not be taped up on the wall, either, of all things. Do people stand on tiptoe or crawl along the floor to read these sheaves of paper? No.

Walls are made for arm-wavers. They set the wrong tone. Writers come to feel that their opus is designed to hang in some gallery, and they actually aim for "design" or "balance" rather than for the winning details of performance, reliability, and life-cycle cost.

## EXPEDITING A LABORIOUS PROCESS

To save days, writers need to finish their storyboards quickly and send them to a cognizant assistant proposal leader. This leader, collaborating perhaps with a competent editor, skims them for technical content (not grammar) and sorts them into *Yes*, *Maybe*, and *No*. Only the *Maybes* need go to the busy proposal manager. The *Yeses* go into writing. (See Figure B.3.)

The *No* storyboards get prompt action of a positive sort. No matter how agonizing the strategic planning has been, some modules inevitably talk too much about the past or address the wrong subject entirely. Others lack detail and need more research. But

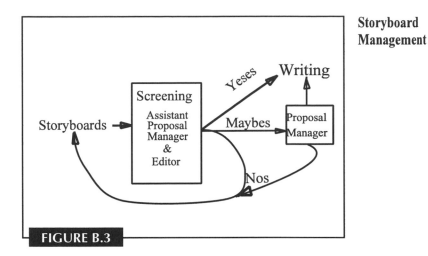

**Storyboard Management**

FIGURE B.3

with attention from managers and editors, even the worst storyboards can enter the writing stage very quickly.

Thus, prewriting can take as little as three days: one for the outline, one for the storyboards, and one for storyboard approval. That's all.

Now, this approach may shock the planning types. But English teachers know the effectiveness of "writing through revision." Spending less time on collaborative sloganeering and more on thoughtful rewrites pays huge dividends; it can give the project two or three extra drafts, each one successively better.

Meanwhile, cognizant management is not left out. It gets a first draft much earlier, with time to make substantive changes to a complete proposal, not just to a hype list of "theme statements."

The review is fast, professional, and intelligent. It gives far more time for detailed, informed planning and redirection. Proposals need such mid-course planning.

Meanwhile, the good writers become available sooner to (1) help the poorer writers, (2) write the executive summary, or, as a treat, (3) help the editors edit. And the whole project bypasses the arm-waving wall-walks and exhausting Hollywood meetings.

## TEACHING ENGINEERS TO WRITE

Contrary to universal claims, engineers are well organized, and their writing, while sometimes clumsy, is not all bad. If left on their own, they will wisely concentrate on facts, rather than on fine words in sonorous "thematic headlines" and "action captions." Amateurs all know that "a proposal is a sales document," but successful editors know that way to sell is not with hype, but with engineering fact.

The marketeers warn about starting to write "too early." This advice is welcomed enthusiastically by the engineers. Traditionally, engineers will do anything to delay writing: one more experiment, one more layout, one more week. If they were writing *Scientific American,* say, or *The National Lampoon,* they'd still be tinkering with the outline to Vol. I, No. 1.

Actually, as suggested by Herb Michaelson, a Fellow of the Society for Technical Communication, authors should begin writing while they are still doing their research! At that point, memory is fresh, detailed, and accurate, and the writing is less painful. Moreover, the writing itself stimulates ideas that lead to further research, which promotes better writing, in an upwardly progressive cycle. (See Figure B.4.)

**Writing Reinforces Research**

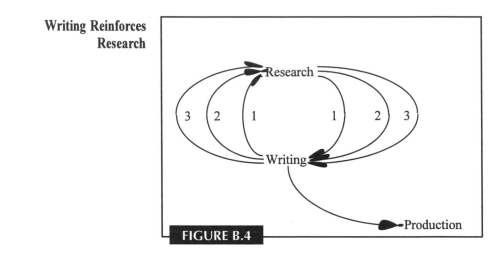

FIGURE B.4

In fact, early writing provides authors at least five benefits:

- The concentration that comes only from actual writing.
- Research that is triggered by questions they find as they write.
- The chemistry of technical collaboration with team members.
- Informed criticism from cognizant management, who are working not from outlines but from complete preliminary drafts.
- Comments from editors, who trim the text, organize thoughts, and emphasize sales points.

## COLLABORATION WITH ARTISTS

An editor should start early to get the author to illustrate every point. The best way to seduce the proposal evaluators is to use enticing, explicit art, not blocks of shouting, boldface word charts. A goal of 50 percent pictures will make your proposal far more meaningful to the poor evaluator who is chained to the copy.

On the other hand, modern-day proposals have become overstuffed with icons, message boxes, and black headlines in a mixture of fonts. Editors need to make proposals clean. As we have said before, one clear word is worth a thousand cluttered pictures.

Some marketeers recommend dummying up pages first and writing the text to fit. But this is manifestly backwards. "Writing to space limitations is good discipline," say the marketeers. But if the editors are any good they are going to chop the text anyway.

And besides, management should leave layout to the artwork professionals.

## IT'S EASIER TO TALK THAN TO WRITE

The prewriting process is never as effective as promised. Teachers know that. Imagine giving a class a master outline—no matter how detailed—and trying to bale up the responding belles lettres into a single coherent document.

The marketeers know that, too; they seldom wait around. They collect their fees and let someone else gather up the scattered shards of the prewriting process and reconcile all the diversities in approach, style, detail, and even simple length, including false starts, wordiness, deadwood, and repetition.

Reconciliation is the job for the editors. As that unwieldy flood of bumbling papers begins to pour in, they relearn the advantage of early writing. It saves days at the start and gives them back when you really need them.

Besides, in proposal efforts, editors find that nearly all of the quality writing comes at the end. Those early, overcrowded storyboard reviews determine only the lowest common denominator of slogans and bombast. The good stuff surfaces later, at a much higher level, frequently coming from talented individual engineers who volunteer to rewrite tangled sections.

## THE EDITING TASK

Good editors don't just chase grammar and consistency; they organize the argument, redirect the thrust, integrate the message, and smooth out the words. Skilled editing makes the words sing in a way that can never be achieved by factual but tone-deaf writers and eager but off-pitch reviewers. A company never need lose a proposal because "engineers can't write." Good editors can fix that.

But the editors' greatest service is to tighten up the message. Drafts generally come in too long. As hard as it is to get engineers to start writing, it's even harder to get them to stop; they treat page "ceilings" as a floor, upon which they typically build an extra 50 percent.

However, this is not bad; it's good. Editors can now spend the days saved earlier to cut the spongy wordiness, adding hard details and new ideas. Herman Holtz (1986) urges us not to write a proposal to a page limit, but to edit it down to that limit. Such "bushwhacking" is routine on magazines that people pay money to read.

Did you ever wonder why professional magazines, with their killing deadlines, don't resort to walls, themes, and storyboards?

## THE EDITOR AS A WRITING EXPERT

Proposal editors can help writers enormously to make their points, and thus to put a winning spin on the final product.

The problem is this. Proposal efforts tend to be dominated by amateur salespeople. Strangely, even though technical people earn their livings by finding facts, the "will to win" pressure often drives them into wild exaggerations and purple prose.

Thus, a courageous editor can become a leader, helping turn the hype back into facts. In fact, as we have said before, editors and engineers may have a reversal of roles, the engineer striving for salesy locutions and the editor guarding against errors in math, both of them working at the job for which they are least well equipped.

The editor should participate in the kickoff meeting, ideally trying to get the team to analyze not just the company benefits in the proposal, but also the company disadvantages. Explaining the company's disadvantages adds credibility to your sales pitch. And besides, if you really do have a disadvatage, you had better explain it thoroughly, not just hope that it goes away. Never be afraid to discuss potential problems; it's a chance to demonstrate your company's experience, with carefully planned fall-back plans.

Another, related idea is to take a crack at attacking the competition's advantages. Too many technical people are scared to bring that up. "You're giving away the store," they argue. But the competition certainly won't hesitate. Don't let them win by default.

A skilled editor can minimize the advantages of the competition by deftly helping clumsy writers plant oblique little messages about worker safety, environmental impact requirements, undocumented labor, or other problems your company perceives in the rival designs (as you know them.) Amateur writers need plenty of help; they are at their worst when they try to be subtle.

## NEAR THE DEADLINE

In short, when working on proposals, active editors can perform their assigned roles of checking spelling, grammar, and consistency. But they can perform other tasks, too, that are infinitely more valuable: As the resident writers on the project, they can help decide the "discriminators," fashion the outline, write the executive summary, create factual beginnings for each section, and slash heavily the resurgent hype to get the proposal down to its page limits. This is a useful occupation, and a lot more fun than checking wiring diagrams.

However, an editor can't always perform this function if she has to spend her time going to marketeering meetings, taping drafts up on the wall, and, in the last days, formatting useless headlines, just because in the frantic chaos there is no time left to do anything else.

Too often, close to the deadline, a proposal project may degenerate into a slogan-writing contest, where collaborative teams vie to turn out the most bombastic headlines. These literary creations have nothing to do with the real world—

"XYZCO serves the user first!"—but too many otherwise intelligent supervisors may think that the customer, even with his rigid list of requirements and his checkoff sheets, will be impressed by sloganeering.

When authors finish their own work, instead of writing bombastic headlines, they should read the proposal text: they might find that the avionics design has removed one of the engines. Editors occasionally find such gaffes, since they read everybody's copy.

## THE BOTTOM LINE

To sum up, contrary to popular opinion, the best proposals result from starting to write early. It saves you days, and allows time for reasoned development of management ideas and skilled revisions by accomplished editors. The finished documents become both more factual and more persuasive.

But don't expect your finished proposal to bear much resemblance to your strategic plan. It will invariably be much better.

# APPENDIX

## About Style Manuals

A "style manual," as most editors well know, has nothing to do with the literary style of Jane Austen or Ernest Hemingway; instead, it is a compilation of the nuts-and-bolts rules for writing, such as abbreviations, capitalizations, and hyphenations, which legitimately vary from publication to publication.

For details, most technical editors consult either *The Chicago Manual of Style* (University of Chicago Press, currently in its 14th edition, 1993) or the *U.S. Government Printing Office Style Manual* (Washington, DC, 1973).

Another good book is Skillin, Marjorie E., and Gay, Robert M., *Words into Type* (Englewood Cliffs, NJ: Prentice-Hall, 1974). Academics follow the *MLA Handbook for Writers of Research Papers* (New York: Modern Language Association of America) or, in recent years, the *Publication Manual of the American Psychological Association* (Washington, DC). Technical people use *Abbreviations for Scientific and Engineering Terms* (New York: American Standards Association) or the publications of the American Institute of Physics (New York).

But most companies also publish their own style manuals. The goal is consistency. The benefit to authors and editors is to prevent having to make style decisions with every article, or even every paragraph or every line. If done right, style manuals can be great savers of time and labor.

Style manuals also prevent embarrassing errors in the treatment of women, minorities, or ethnic or religious groups. They aim at stomping out derogatory ethnic or gender terms. The good ones have tips on writing, largely in the direction of succinctness.

For an editor, newspaper style manuals are fun to browse. Can you use *Fannie Mae* outside of the financial pages? Which is right, *Farsi* or *Persian*? Can you speak of a *Filipino* woman? Do you hyphen *first-baseman*? What's the difference between *plush* and *posh*?

Technical writing has its own style. We omit capitals and periods in most abbreviations of units of measure (ft). On quantities of less than unity we put a zero in front of the decimal point (0.25). We often say we prefer a "down" style, but we use an enormous number of initial caps.

## THE PROBLEMS

But, despite their advantages, style manuals could be the death of technical editing. They are dominating the profession and usurping enormous amounts of time, requiring endless meetings and repeated updates and rewrites.

Proponents say "take care of the little things, and the big things will take care of themselves." Actually, while technical editors are making war on -*ize*, those really big things, like logic and technical accuracy, may be neglected entirely. A course on "advanced editing" at the University of California at San Diego advertises, among its principal topics, selecting a style manual and making lists of prohibited words.

Style manuals do appeal to the technical mind. The director of research for a major company once called in the chief editor and said, "What we need is a style manual." The editor asked, "If I wrote one, would you follow it?" The director caught the point immediately. His eyes twinkled as he smiled, "I would if it was a good one."

In major companies, the problem of consistency may be largely unreconcilable. The public relations department has to use a "down" style because it is writing for newspapers, but department heads insist on capitalizing the names of titles and departments. advanced design prefers *data is*, but the laboratory is firm for *data are*. The Navy style differs significantly from that of NASA or the Air Force. What does an editor do? Compel compliance? Hold more meetings?

Thus, a monolithic corporate style manual may not be the way to go. It cannot solve all of the above problems, no matter how much it uses weasel words. In technical writing, "consistency" is far from being our greatest problem. Besides, editors run into resistance from authors who say, "If it ain't in the manual, I ain't changing it."

One practical solution is to compile brief style lists for separate purposes. For example, editors of proposals should make a quick run through the RFP to determine customer preferences and publish a list for the word processors (who in most companies are the best guardians of style). Departments should be free to compile their own lists to take care of special circumstances.

The operative word is *brief*. Style manuals more and more are becoming second-rate grammar books, full of personal prohibitions and pet peeves. On the other hand, many of them surprisingly do not make decisions, but rather say "it depends." The purpose of a style manual is to set down rules, not to list the TBDs.

The editors of the *New York Times,* sticklers for style, have put a note in the front of their *Manual of Style and Usage:* "Style rules should not be so extensive as to inhibit the writer or the editor. The rules should encourage thinking, not discourage it. A single rule might suffice: 'The rule of common sense will prevail at all times.'"

# APPENDIX
# D

## Bibliography of Cited and Other Useful Sources

Aiken, Janet Rankin. (1936) *Commonsense Grammar.* New York: Crowell.

*American Heritage Dictionary of the English Language, The.* (1969) Edited by William Morris. Boston: American Heritage Publishing Co. & Houghton Mifflin.

———. (1992) 3rd ed. Boston: Houghton Mifflin.

*AIP Style Manual*, (1990) 4th ed. New York: American Institute of Physics.

Amsden, Dorothy C. (1980) "Get in the Habit of Editing Illustrations." *Proceedings of the 27th International Technical Communication Conference (ITCC).* Minneapolis, May 14–17. Arlington, VA: Society for Technical Communication.

———. (1982) "Exercise Your Visual Thinking." *Proceedings of the 29th International Technical Communication Conference (ITCC).* Boston, May 5–8.

Annett, Clarence H. (1985) "Improving Communication: Eleven Guidelines for the New Technical Editor." *Journal of Technical Writing and Communication* 15(2), 175–79.

Armour, Richard. (1969) *On Your Marks.* New York: McGraw-Hill.

Baker, Robert A., ed. (1963) *Stress Analysis of a Strapless Evening Gown.* Englewood Cliffs, NJ: Prentice Hall.

Ball, Alice Morton. (1939) *Compounding in the English Language.* New York: Wilson.

Baron, Dennis. (1992) "Why Do Academics Continue to Insist on 'Proper English'?" *The Chronicle of Higher Education,* 1 July: B1–2. Responses, 29 July: B3.

Baron, Dennis E. (1982) *Grammar and Good Taste: Reforming the American Language.* New Haven: Yale University Press.

Barzun, Jacques. (1986) "Behind the Blue Pencil: Censorship or Creeping Creativity?" *On Writing, Editing, and Publishing: Essays, Explicative and Hortatory.* Chicago: University of Chicago Press.

Baugh, Albert C. (1935) *History of the English Language.* New York: Appleton.

Bernstein, Theodore M. (1958) *Watch Your Language: A Lively, Informal Guide to Better Writing, Emanating from the News Room of the New York Times.* Great Neck, NY: Channel Press.

————. (1965) *The Careful Writer: A Modern Guide to English Usage.* New York: Atheneum.

————. (1971) *Miss Thistlebottom's Hobgoblins: The Careful Writer's Guide to the Taboos, Bugbears and Outmoded Rules of English Usage.* New York: Simon and Schuster.

*Blair Handbook, The.* See under Fulwiler, Toby.

Blair, Hugh. (1783) *Lectures on Rhetoric and Belles Lettres.* 2 vols. Edited by Harold F. Harding. Carbondale: Southern Illinois University Press, Reprint, 1965.

Brogan, John A. (1973) *Clear Technical Writing.* New York: McGraw-Hill.

Brown, Marshall. (1893) *Bulls and Blunders.* Chicago: S. C. Griggs.

Bryson, Bill. (1990) *The Mother Tongue.* New York: Morrow.

Buehler, Mary F. (1981) "Defining Terms in Technical Editing: The Levels of Edit as a Model." *Technical Communication* 28(4) 10–14.

Burchfield, Robert. (1991) *Unlocking the English Language.* 1st Am. ed. N.p.: Hill and Wang.

Bush, Don. (1994) "Chopping Copy." *Technical Communication* 41(2) 322–24.

————. (1993) "Let the Authors Have Their Words." *Technical Communication* 40 (1) 125–28.

————. (1992) "The Technology of Human Editing." *Technical Communication* 39(1) 115–16.

————. (1991) "What Are Editors Worth?" *Technical Communication* 38(3) 386.

————. (1981) "Content Editing, an Opportunity for Growth." *Technical Communication* 28(4) 15–18.

Campbell, Charles P. (1992) "Engineering Style: Striving for Efficiency." *IEEE Transactions on Professional Communication* 35: 130–37.

Campbell, George. (1776) *The Philosophy of Rhetoric.* New York: J. Leavitt, Reprint, 1834.

Campbell, Walter S. (1950) *Writing: Advice and Devices.* Garden City, NY: Doubleday.

*Chicago Manual of Style, The.* (1993) 14th ed. Chicago: University of Chicago Press.

Chomsky, Noam. (1957) *Syntactic Structures.* The Hague, The Netherlands: Mouton..

Christensen, Francis. (1978) *Notes Toward a New Rhetoric.* 2nd ed. New York: Harper & Row.

Ciardi, John. (1980) *A Browser's Dictionary: A Compendium of Curious Expressions and Intriguing Facts.* New York: Harper & Row.

————. (1983) *A Second Browser's Dictionary, and Native's Guide to the Unknown American Language.* New York: Harper & Row.

Cook, Claire Kehrwald. (1985) *Line by Line: How to Improve Your Own Writing.* Boston: Houghton Mifflin.

Crabtree, Monica, and Joyce Powers, comps. (1991) *Language Files.* 5th ed. Columbus, OH: Ohio State University.

Finegan, Edward. (1980) *Attitudes Toward English Usage.* New York: Teachers College Press.

Flesch, Rudolf. (1943) *The Marks of Readable Style.* New York: Teachers College Press.

————. (1946) *The Art of Plain Talk.* 3rd ed. New York: Harper.

————. (1949) *The Art of Readable Writing.* New York: Harper.

Fowler, H. Ramsey, Jane E. Aaron, and Kay Limburg. (1992) *The Little, Brown Handbook.* 5th ed. New York: HarperCollins.

Fowler, H. W., and F. G. Fowler. (1907) *The King's English.* Oxford: Clarendon.

Fowler, H. W., and Sir Ernest Gowers. (1965) *A Dictionary of Modern English Usage.* 2nd ed. New York: Oxford University Press.

Fulwiler, Toby, and Alan R. Hayakawa. (1994) *The Blair Handbook.* Englewood Cliffs, NJ: Prentice Hall.

Gallagher, William J. (1969) *Report Writing for Management.* Reading, MA: Addison-Wesley.

Gopen, George, and Judith Swan. (1990) "The Science of Scientific Writing." *American Scientist* 78: 550–55.

GPO Style Manual. See *U. S. Government Printing Office Style Manual.*

Graves, Robert, and Alan Hodge. (1944) *The Reader Over Your Shoulder.* New York: Macmillan.

Green, Tamara M. (1994) *The Greek and Latin Roots of English.* 2nd ed. New York: Ardsley House.

Greenbaum, Sidney. (1988) *Good English and the Grammarian.* London: Longman.

Gross, Gerald, ed. (1993) *Editors on Editing.* 3rd ed. New York: Grove.

Gunning, Robert. (1952) *The Technique of Clear Writing.* New York: McGraw-Hill.

———. (1964) *How to Take the Fog Out of Writing.* Chicago: Dartnell.

*Harbrace College Handbook.* See under Hodges, John C.

Hayakawa, S. I. (1941) *Language in Action.* New York: Harcourt, Brace.

———. (1964) *Language in Thought and Action.* 2nd ed. NewYork: Harcourt, Brace & World.

Hayakawa, S. I., and Alan R. Hayakawa. (1990) *Language in Thought and Action.* 5th ed. New York: Harcourt Brace Jovanovich.

Hodges, John C., Mary E. Whitten, Winifred B. Horner, Suzanne S. Webb, and Robert K. Miller. (1990) *Harbrace College Handbook.* 11th ed. San Diego: Harcourt Brace Jovanovich.

*Ho-Hum, Newsbreaks from The New Yorker.* (1931) New York: Farrar & Rinehart.

Holtz, Herman. (1986) *The Consultant's Guide to Proposal Writing.* New York: Wiley.

Horton, William K. (1990) *Designing and Writing Online Documentation: Help Files and Hypertext.* New York: Wiley.

———. (1991) *Illustrating Computer Documentation: The Art of Presenting Information Graphically on Paper and Online.* New York: Wiley.

Howard, Philip. (1985) *The State of the Language.* New York: Oxford.

Huff, Darrell. (1954) *How to Lie with Statistics.* New York: Norton.

Hunt, Kellogg. (1965) *Grammatical Structures Written at Three Grade Levels.* Champaign, IL: National Council of Teachers of English.

Jarman, Brian. (1980) "Coping with Crash Editing." *Proceedings of the 27th International Technical Communication Conference (ITCC).* Minneapolis, May 14–17. Arlington, VA: Society for Technical Communication.

Jespersen, Otto. (1926) Society for Pure English, Tract No. XXX. "On Some Disputed Points in English Grammar." Oxford, at the Clarendon Press.

Jodrell, Richard Paul. (1820) *Philology on the English Language.* London: Cox & Baylis.

Judd, Karen. (1990) *Copyediting: A Practical Guide.* 2nd ed. Los Altos, CA: Crisp.

Kaplan, Jeffrey P. (1989) *English Grammar, Principles and Facts.* Englewood Cliffs, NJ: Prentice Hall.

Killingsworth, M. Jimmie, and Michael K. Gilbertson. (1992) *Signs, Genres, and Communities in Technical Communication.* Amityville, NY: Baywood.

Kolln, Martha. (1994) *Understanding English Grammar.* 4th ed. New York: Macmillan.

"Last Word in Words." (1993) *Los Angeles Times,* 20 September.

Leonard, Sterling. (1929) *The Doctrine of Correctness in English Usage, 1700–1800.* Madison: University of Wisconsin.

Linton, Calvin. (1961) *Effective Revenue Writing.* Washington, DC: U.S. Government Printing Office.

*Literary Market Place.* (Annual) Ann Arbor, MI: R. R. Bowker.

*Little, Brown Handbook, The.* See under Fowler, H. Ramsey.

*MLA Handbook for Writers of Research Papers.* (1988) 3rd ed. New York: Modern Language Association of America.

McArthur, Tom, ed. (1992) *The Oxford Companion to the English Language.* New York: Oxford University Press.

McCrum, Robert, William Cran, and Robert MacNeil. (1986) *The Story of English.* New York: Viking.

Marckwardt, Albert H. (1958) *American English.* New York: Oxford University Press.

Marckwardt, Albert H., and J. L. Dillard. (1980) *American English.* 2nd ed. New York: Oxford University Press.

Mathes, J. C., and Dwight W. Stevenson. (1991) *Designing Technical Reports.* 2nd ed. New York: Macmillan.

Medawar, P. B. (1964) "Is the Scientific Paper Fraudulent? Yes; It Misrepresents Scientific Thought." *Saturday Review,* 1 August, 42–43.

Meyers, Walter E. (1980) *Aliens and Linguists: Language Study and Science Fiction.* Athens, GA: University of Georgia Press.

Michaels, Leonard, and Christopher Ricks, eds. (1980) *The State of the Language.* Berkeley: University of California Press.

Mitchell, Richard. (1979) *Less Than Words Can Say.* Boston: Little, Brown.

———. (1984) *The Leaning Tower of Babel and Other Affronts by the Underground Grammarian.* Boston: Little, Brown.

Moore, John. (1962) *You English Words.* Philadelphia: Lippincott.

Morenberg, Max. (1991) *Doing Grammar.* New York: Oxford.

Ogden, C. K., and I. A. Richards. (1930) *The Meaning of Meaning.* New York: Harcourt, Brace.

Ogilvy, David. (1983) *Ogilvy on Advertising.* New York: Crown.

O'Neill, Carol L., and Avima Ruder. (1979) *The Complete Guide to Editorial Freelancing.* New York: Barnes and Noble.

Ong, Walter J. (1944) "Historical Backgrounds of Elizabethan and Jacobean Punctuation Theory." *PMLA* 59: 349–60.

———. (1982) *Orality and Literacy: The Technologizing of the Word.* New York: Methuen.

*Oxford Companion to the English Language, The.* See under McArthur, Tom.

*Oxford English Dictionary, The.* (1989) 2nd ed. New York: Oxford University Press.

*Pocket Pal: A Graphic Arts Production Handbook.* (1983) 13th ed. New York: International Paper Co.

Price, Jonathan. (1984) *How to Write a Computer Manual: A Handbook of Software Documentation.* Menlo Park, CA: Benjamin/Cummings.

Price, Jonathan, and Henry Korman. (1993) *How to Communicate Technical Information: A Handbook of Software and Hardware Documentation.* Redwood City, CA: Benjamin/Cummings.

*Publication Manual of the American Psychological Association.* (1983) 3rd ed. Washington, DC: The Association.

Putnam, Constance E. (1985) "Myths about Editing." *Technical Communication* 32(2) 17–20.

Quinn, Jim. (1980) *American Tongue and Cheek.* New York: Pantheon.

Rapoport, Anatol. (1954) *Operational Philosophy.* New York: Harper.

Read, Allen Walker. (1989) "'At Play in the Language': Interview with Michelle Stacey." *New Yorker.* 4 September.

Riblet, Carl, Jr. (1974) *The Solid Gold Copy Editor.* Chicago: Aldine.

Rickard, T. A. (1910) *A Guide to Technical Writing.* 2nd ed. San Francisco: Mining & Scientific Press.

Rook, Fern. (1992) *Slaying the English Jargon.* Arlington, VA: The Society for Technical Communication, 1992.

Rude, Carolyn. (1991) *Technical Editing.* Belmont, CA: Wadsworth.

Safire, William. (1994) "On Language." *New York Times,* 29 August.

———. (1993) Sept. 12.

Sapir, Edward. (1921) *Language: An Introduction to the Study of Speech.* New York: Harcourt.

Shidle, Norman. (1951) *Clear Writing Makes Easy Reading.* New York: McGraw-Hill.

Simon, John. (1980) *Paradigms Lost: Reflections on Literacy and Its Decline.* New York: C. N. Potter.

Skillin, Marjorie E., and Robert M. Gay. (1974) *Words into Type.* Englewood Cliffs, NJ: Prentice Hall.

Snow, C. P. (1959) *The Two Cultures and the Scientific Revolution.* New York: Cambridge University Press.

Strunk, William, and E. B. White. (1979) *The Elements of Style.* 3rd. ed. New York: Macmillan.

Swan, Michael. (1981) *Practical English Usage.* New York: Oxford University Press.

Tarutz, Judith A. (1992) *Technical Editing: The Practical Guide for Editors and Writers.* Reading, MA: Addison-Wesley. 105–08, 249–50.

Teall, Horace. (1891) *The Compounding of English Words.* New York: John Ireland.

Tichy, Henrietta, and Sylvia Fourdrinier. (1988) *Effective Writing for Engineers, Managers, Scientists.* 2nd ed. New York: Wiley.

Tufte, Edward R. (1983) *The Visual Display of Quantitative Information.* Cheshire, CT: Graphics Press.

———. (1990) *Envisioning Information.* Cheshire, CT: Graphics Press.

*U.S. Government Printing Office Style Manual.* (1973) Rev. ed. Washington, DC: U.S. Government Printing Office.

*Verbatim, Volumes I and II.* (1978) Essex, CT: Verbatim, The Language Quarterly.

Visco, Louis J. (1981) *The Manager as an Editor: Reviewing Memos, Letters, and Reports.* Boston: CBI Publishing Company.

Walpole, Jane R. (1979) "Why Must the Passive Be Damned?" *College Composition and Communication* 30: 3.

Walsh, William S. (1911) *Handy-Book of Literary Curiosities.* Philadelphia: Lippincott.

Weber, Robert. L., ed. (1973) *A Random Walk in Science: An Anthology.* New York: Crane, Russak.

*Webster's Dictionary of English Usage.* (1989). Springfield, MA: Merriam-Webster.

*Webster's Third New International Dictionary of the English Language.* (1961). Springfield, MA: Merriam-Webster.

Weekley, Ernest. (1913) *The Romance of Words.* 2nd ed. New York: Dutton.

Weiss, Edmond H. (1990) *100 Writing Remedies.* Phoenix: Oryx Press.

———. (1991) *How to Write Usable User Documentation.* 2nd ed. Phoenix: Oryx Press.

White, Jan V. (1982) *Editing by Design: A Guide to Effective Word-and-Picture Communication for Editors and Designers.* 2nd ed. New York: Bowker.

———. (1990) *Color for the Electronic Age.* New York: Watson.

———. (1991) *Illustrating Computer Documentation.* New York: Wiley.

Williams, Joseph M. (1981). "The Phenomenology of Error." *College Composition and Communication* 32: 152–68.

———. (1994) *Style: Ten Lessons in Clarity and Grace.* 4th ed. New York: HarperCollins.

Winterowd, W. Ross. (1975) *The Contemporary Writer.* New York: Harcourt Brace Jovanovich.

Zinsser, William. (1988) *On Writing Well.* 3rd ed. New York: Harper & Row.

# INDEX

by Virgil Diodato